Collecting
Toy
Airplanes
An Identification & Valuc Guide
by
Ron smith

ISBN 0-89689-111-9

BOOKS AMERICANA
INC.

TABLE OF CONTENTS

ACKNOWLEDGMENTS

I would like to thank the following people for all the assistance given to me to produce this airplane price guide. To Martin Braunlich who knows his airplanes inside and out. Many an evening and many brewskis went into photographing diecast airplanes and labeling unidentified Japanese tin plane photos. To Bruce Kullik who supplied many tin jets and all the tin helicopters contained here. To my Swiss friend Rodney Abensur of Geneva, Switzerland for the photos of so many Rico and Paya tin aircraft. To Rich and Faith Savage who I have known longer than I care to remember, 32 years. Their boxed sets of Tootsietoy airplanes are a joy to look at. Lastly to Dan Alexander and Don Hultzman for the push to get started on this project and to my wife Joannie for leaving me alone long enough to get it done.

P.S. I almost forgot a long lost trading buddy who years ago supplied me with photos of Japanese tin airplanes. Mr. Tanaka hopefully doing well somewhere in Tokyo, Japan.

AERO MINI
Die Cast

Incorporated in 1968 these precision made diecast scale model airplanes were initially manufactured in the United States then transferred the manufacturing to a Japanese toy company in about 1970. Production ceased in 1976 after one half million planes were produced.

(N.P.F. - NO PRICE FOUND)

	MAN #	TYPE	AIRLINE/COUNTRY	C6	C8	C10
AM 1	3006	A6M5 ZERO	JAPAN NAVY (GREEN)	125	175	250
AM 2	3006	A6M5 ZERO	JAPAN NAVY (SILVER)	150	200	300
AM 3	7001	BOEING 707	PAN AM	30	50	75
AM 4	7002	BOEING 707	TWA	30	50	75
AM 5	7003	BOEING 707	NORTHWEST ORIENT	30	50	75
AM 6	7005	BOEING 707	AMERICAN	35	60	85
AM 7	7201	BOEING 727	PAN AM	30	60	70
AM 8	7202	BOEING 727	TWA	30	50	75
AM 9	7203	BOEING 727	NORTHWEST ORIENT	30	50	75
AM 10	7204	BOEING 727	J.A.L.	90	125	175
AM 11	7205	BOEING 727	AMERICAN	30	50	75
AM 12	7207	BOEING 727	EASTERN	30	50	75
AM 13	7210	BOEING 727	BRANIFF (RED)	40	60	90
AM 14	7210	BOEING 727	BRANIFF (BLUE)	30	50	75
AM 15	7274	BOEING 727	ALL NIPPON	90	125	175
AM 16	7306	BOEING 737	UNITED	20	30	40
AM 17	7316	BOEING 737	PIEDMONT	30	40	50
AM 18	7379	BOEING 737	ALL NIPPON	90	125	150
AM 19	7400	BOEING 747	BOEING DASH-100	N. P. F.		
AM 20	7401	BOEING 747	PAN AM	60	90	125
AM 21	7402	BOEING 747	TWA	60	90	125
AM 22	7403	BOEING 747	NORTHWEST ORIENT	90	125	150
AM23	7404	BOEING 747	J.A.L.	150	250	300
AM 24	7405	BOEING 747	AMERICAN	90	125	150
AM 25	7405C	BOEING 747	CHROMED AMERICAN	N. P. F.		
AM 26	7407	BOEING 747	EASTERN	90	125	150
AM 27	7409	BOEING 747	BOAC	150	250	300
AM 28	7413	BOEING 747	AIR CANADA	150	250	300
AM 29	7451	BOEING 747	SPIRIT OF 76	N. P. F.		
AM 30	7451	BOEING 747	USAF E4A	N. P. F.		
AM 31	7051	BOEING C-135	USAF	N. P. F.		
AM 32	7051	BOEING C-135	USAF (BLACK NOSE)	N. P. F.		
AM 33	8004	DC-8	JAL	150	250	300
AM 34	8007	DC-8	EASTERN	100	200	250
AM 35	8013	DC-8	AIR CANADA	100	200	250
AM 36	9002	DC-9	TWA	20	30	40
AM 37	9007	DC-9	EASTERN	20	30	40
AM 38	9008	DC-9	OZARK	20	30	40
AM 39	9013	DC-9	AIR CANADA	20	30	40
AM 40	4251	F-104J	USAF	90	125	150
AM 41	4257	F-104J	GERMAN AIR FORCE	90	125	150

					C6	C8	C10
AM 42	4150	F-4E PHANTOM	USN (SILVER)		90	125	150
AM 43	4150	F-4E PHANTOM	USN (GRAY)		90	125	150
AM 44	4151	F-4E PHANTOM	USAF		90	125	150
AM 45	4152	F-4E PHANTOM	ROYAL NAVY		90	125	150
AM 46	4156	F-4E PHANTOM	JAPANESE AIR FORCE		150	250	300
AM 47	2009	SUPER VC-10	BOAC		60	90	125

AM 1

AM3

AM9

AM14

AM15

AM21

AM28

AM34

AM45

AM38

AM47

AHM SHOWCASE MINIATURES
1:100 Scale Plastic

	MAN #	TYPE	C6	C8	C10
AHM 1	SM-1	CURTISS P-6E BIPLANE	10	20	30
AHM 2	SM-2	GRUMMAN F3F-3 BIPLANE	10	20	30
AHM 3	SM-3	BOEING F4B-4 BIPLANE	10	20	30
AHM 4	SM-4	BOEING P-26A	10	20	30
AHM 5	SM-5	N.A	10	20	30
AHM 6	SM-6	WINNIE MAE	10	20	30
AHM 7	SM-7	ZERO A6M5	10	20	30
AHM 8	SM-8	HEIN TONY Ki-61-1	10	20	30
AHM 9	SM-9	NA-P51D MUSTANG	10	20	30
AHM 10	SM-10	ME 109E	10	20	30
AHM 11	SM-11	NA P51D MISS AMERICA	15	25	35
AHM 12	SM-12	CURTISS P 40E FLYING TIGER	10	20	30
AHM 13	SM-13	BELL P 39 AIRACOBRA	10	20	30
		1:87 SCALE PLASTIC			
AHM 14	SM-14	MCDONNELL DOUGLAS F4E PHANTOM II	30	40	50
AHM 15	SM-15	LOCKHEED P 38 LIGHTNING	30	40	50
AHM 16	SM-16	JUNKER JU 87 G STUKA	30	40	50

AHM 2

Grumman F3F-3
Accurate Scale • Authentic Insignia • Movable Control Surfaces

AHM 3

Boeing F4B-4
Accurate Scale • Authentic Insignia • Movable Control Surfaces

AHM 6

Winnie Mae
Accurate Scale • Authentic Insignia • Movable Control Surfaces

AHM 8

Hein Tony K1-61-1
Accurate Scale • Authentic Insignia • Movable Control Surfaces

AHM 9

NA P-51D Mustang
Accurate Scale • Authentic Insignia • Movable Control Surfaces

AHM 10

ME-BF109E
Accurate Scale • Authentic Insignia • Movable Control Surfaces

AHM 11

N.A. P-51D MISS AMERICA
Accurate Scale • Authentic Insignia • Movable Control Surfaces

AHM 12

CURTISS P-40E FLYING TIGER
Accurate Scale • Authentic Insignia • Movable Control Surfaces

AHM 13

BELL P-39 AIRACOBRA
Accurate Scale • Authentic Insignia • Movable Control Surfaces

AHM 14

AHM 15

AHM 16

BACHMAN MINI AIRCRAFT
Plastic—Assorted Scales

Manufactured by Bachman Bros. Inc. of Philadelphia, Pa. Production started in the late 60s and ceased in the mid-80s. Original production was in a nonwindow box, later it was changed to a window box and finally to a blister card.

	MAN #	TYPE	SCALE	C6	C8	C10
BM 1	8001	P-40 FLYING TIGER	1:160	5	10	20
BM 2	8002	MESSERSCHMITT ME-109	1:160	5	10	20
BM 3	8003	MIG-19	1:200	5	10	20
BM 4	8003	MIG-21C	1:200	5	10	20
BM 5	8004	F-104 STARFIGHTER	1:210	5	10	20
BM 6	8005	FRENCH MIRAGE 4A	1:270	5	10	20
BM 7	8006	B-17 FLYING FORTRESS	1:250	5	10	20
BM 8	8007	BRITISH SPITFIRE	1:140	5	10	20
BM 9	8008	JAPANESE ZERO	1:140	5	10	20
BM 10	8009	BOEING 707 TWA	1:440	5	10	20
BM 11	8009	BOEING 707 AMERICAN	1:440	5	10	20
BM 12	8009	BOEING 707 PAN AMERICAN	1.440	5	10	20
BM 13	8010	THUNDERCHIEF F-105	1:240	5	10	20
BM 14	8011	MUSTANG P-51	1:150	5	10	20
BM 15	8012	LIGHTNING P-38	1:160	5	10	20
BM 16	8013	BELL AH-IG HUEYCOBRA	1:210	5	10	20
BM 17	8014	MITCHELL B-25	1:190	5	10	20
BM 18	8015	CORSAIR F-4U	1:160	5	10	20
BM 19	8016	SPIRIT OF ST LOUIS	1:90	5	10	20
BM 20	8017	FOKKER DR-1	1:90	5	10	20
BM 21	8018	SPAD XIII	1:100	5	10	20
BM 22	8019	CONVAIR 880 TWA	1:400	5	10	20
BM 23	8019	CONVAIR 880 DELTA	1:400	5	10	20
BM 24	8020	SOPWITH CAMEL	1:90	5	10	20
BM 25	8021	ALBATROS D-III	1:110	5	10	20
BM 26	8022	BOEING 727 EASTERN	1:410	5	10	20
BM 27	8022	BOEING 727 UNITED	1:410	5	10	20
BM 28	8023	DOUGLAS DC-9 EASTERN	1:290	5	10	20
BM 29	8023	DOUGLAS DC-9 TWA	1:290	5	10	20
BM 30	8023	DOUGLAS DC-9 DELTA	1:290	5	10	20
BM 31	8324	F-4K PHANTOM BRITISH	1:125	5	10	20
BM 32	8325	DOUGLAS DC-8JAL	1:450	5	10	20
BM 33	8325	DOUGLAS DC-8 UNITED	1:450	5	10	20
BM 34	8326	LOCKHEED YF-12A	1:340	5	10	20
BM 35	8327	JUNKERS JU-88	1:170	5	10	20
BM 36	8328	LANCASTER	1:240	5	10	20
BM 37	8329	NEUPORT 17	1:90	5	10	20
BM 38	8330	FOKKER EINDECKER E III	1:110	5	10	20
BM 39	8331	STUKA JU-87	1:160	5	10	20

	MAN #	TYPE	SCALE	C6	C8	C10
BM 40	8332	P-47 D THUNDERBOLT	1:160	5	10	20
BM 41	8333	FOKKER D-VII	1:100	5	10	20
BM 42	8334	S.E.5A	1:100	5	10	20
BM 43	8335	BOEING 747 PAN AM	1:450	5	10	20
BM 44	8335	BOEING 747 JAL	1:450	5	10	20
BM 45	8335	BOEING 747 UNITED	1:450	5	10	20
BM 46	8336	BOEING F4B-4	1:100	5	10	20
BM 47	8337	WRIGHT BROTHERS KITTY HAWK	1:100	5	10	20
BM 48	8338	SIKORSKY HH-3E JOLLY GREEN GIANT	1:260	5	10	20
BM 49	8339	B-24 LIBERATOR	1:340	5	10	20
BM 50	8340	DC-10 AMERICAN	1:100	5	10	20
BM 51	8341	SAAB AJ37 VIGGEN	1:200	5	10	20
BM 52	8342	CURTISS P-6E HAWK	1:100	5	10	20
BM 53	8343	FORD TRI-MOTOR	1:200	5	10	20
BM 54	8344	PBY-5A CATALINA	1:340	5	10	20
BM 55	8345	C-119 FLYING BOX CAR	1:280	5	10	20
BM 56	8346	NAKAJIMA Ki-44-2 SHOKI	1:130	30	40	50
BM 57	8347	KAWANISHI N1K1 KYOFU	1:140	30	40	50
BM 58	8348	MITSUBISHI Ki-21 TYPE 97 BOMBER	1:250	30	40	50
BM 59	8349	HEIN 2 FIGHTER ''TONY''	1:145	30	40	50
BM 60	8350	YOKOSUKA P1Y1 ''FRANCIS''	1:190	30	40	50
BM 61	8351	NAKAJIMA Ki-43 "OSCAR"	1:130	30	40	50
BM 62	8352	NAKAJIMA B5N ''KATE''	1:170	30	40	50
BM 63	8353	NAMC YS-11	1:170	5	10	20
BM 64	8354	MITSUBISHI MU-2B	1:130	5	10	20
BM 65	8355	OS2U-3 KINGFISHER	1:160	5	10	20
BM 66	8356	KAWANISHI NiK2-J SHIDENKAI "GEORGE"	1:145	30	40	50
BM 67	8357	MITSUBISHI J2M3 RAIDEN ''JACK''	1:150	30	40	50
BM 68	8358	MITSUBISHI Ki-46-3 RECON "DINAH"	1:170	5	10	20
BM 69	8359	MITSUBISHI G4M2 ''BETTY''	1:260	5	10	20
BM 70	8360	KAWANISHI H8K2 FLYING BOAT ''EMILY''	1:310	5	10	20
BM 71	8361	POLIKARPOV	1:100	5	10	20
BM 72	8362	GRUMMAN F4F WILDCAT	1:140	5	10	20
BM 73	8363	FOCKE-WULF 190	1:140	5	10	20
BM 74	8364	MORAINE SAULNIER	1:100	5	10	20
BM 75	8365	B-58 HUSTLER	1:260	5	10	20
BM 76	8366	DOUGLAS SKYRAIDER	1:160	5	10	20
BM 77	8367	GRUMMAN F3F	1:100	5	10	20
BM 78	8368	B-29 SUPER FORTRESS	1:380	5	10	20
BM 79	8369	BELL UH 1B IROQUOIS	1:200	5	10	20
BM 80	8370	CURTISS HELLDIVER	1:160	5	10	20
BM 81	8371	MOSQUITO	1:160	5	10	20
BM 82	8372	DOUGLAS DC-3 AMERICAN	1:280	5	10	20
BM 83	8373	GEE BEE RACER	1:180	5	10	20
BM 84	8374	WESTLAND LYSANDER	1:100	5	10	20
BM 85	8375	DORNIER DO-17	1:170	5	10	20
BM 86	8376	HAWKER HURRICANE IIC	1:160	5	10	20
BM 87	8377	GRUMMAN HAWKEYE	1:210	5	10	20
BM 88	8378	DOUGLAS A-4 SKYHAWK	1:125	5	10	20

	MAN#	TYPE	SCALE	C6	C8	C10
BM 89	8379	KAMIKAZE		30	40	50
BM 90	8380	AICHI TYPE 99 "VAL"		30	40	50
BM 91	8381	JAPANESE KITSUKA	1:105	30	40	50
BM 92	8382	FUGI FA-200 AERO SUBARU		30	40	50
BM 93	8383	SHINMEIWA PS-1 FLYING BOAT		30	40	50
BM 94	8384	KAWASKI/BOEING VERTOL V107		30	40	50
BM 95	8388	LOCKHEED C-130 HERCULES	1:400	5	10	20
BM 96	8389	OV-10A NORTH AMERICAN "BRONCO"	1:160	5	10	20
BM 97	8390	P-51 MUSTANG	1:150	5	10	20
BM 98	8391	PHANTOM F-4K (BLUE ANGELS)	1:125	5	10	20
BM 99	8392	P-47D THUNDERBOLT	1:150	5	10	20
BM 100	8393	HINDENBURG		15	20	25
BM 101	8394	HUGHES HERCULES HK-1	1:850	5	10	20
BM 102	8395	NORTH AMERICAN B-1	1:400	5	10	20
BM 103	8396	F-105 THUNDERCHIEF	1:240	5	10	20
BM 104	8397	P-38 LIGHTNING		5	10	20
BM 105	8398	JUNKERS JU-88		5	10	20
BM 106	8399	TBM AVENGER	1:160	5	10	20
BM 107	8402	BOEING CLIPPER	1:450	5	10	20
BM 108	8403	NORTHROP T-38 TALON "THUNDERBIRD"	1:125	5	10	20
BM 109	8404	BOEING YC-14		30	40	50
BM 110	8405	CONCORDE BRITISH	1:600	5	10	20
BM 111	8406	BRISTOL F2B FIGHTER	1:120	5	10	20
BM 112	8407	SPACE SHUTTLE	1:500	5	10	20

BACHMAN SETS

BM 113	8501	WORLD WAR II SET—6 PLANES P-40, ME-109, B-17, SPITFIRE, ZERO, P-51	—	—	150
BM 114	8502	COMMERCIAL AIRLINERS SET— 4 PLANES 707, 880, 727, DC-9	—	—	120
BM 115	8503	JET FIGHTERS SET—6 PLANES MIG-21C, F-104, F-105, MIRAGE, F-4K, YF-12A	—	—	150
BM 116	8504	WORLD WAR I SERIES 1 SET—4 PLANES FOKKER DR-1, SPAD XIII, ALBATROS, SOPWITH CAMEL	—	—	120
BM 117	8505	HISTORIC AIRCRAFT SET—4 PLANES KITTY HAWK, SPIRIT OF ST. LOUIS, FORD TRI-MOTOR, BOEING 747	—	—	120
BM 118	8506	WORLD WAR I SERIES 2 SET—4 PLANES NIEUPORT 17, SE-5A, FOKKER, FINDECKER, FOKKER D-VII	—	—	120

BM 19

BM 82

BM 99

BM 100

BM 41   **BM 20**

BM 97   **BM 73**

BACHMAN ASSTD. BOXES

DINKY TOYS

Die Cast England and France
From The Collection of Martin Braunlich

Production started in 1933 and continued through the late 30s when World War II brought production to a stop in both England and France. The company changed ownership several times and ceased production in 1988. Dinky Toys made a wide range of toy autos, trucks, airplanes, trains and construction equipment and has always been considered the premier manufacturer of transportation toys.

	MAN #	DESCRIPTION	YR. OF MAN.	C6	C8	C10
DK 1	60A	DEWOITINE "ARC-EN-CIEL"	1935	150	225	300
DK 2	60A	IMPERIAL AIRWAYS LINER	1934	200	300	400
DK 3	60A	MYSTERE IV A	1957	50	75	100
DK 4	60B	POTEZ 58	1935	150	225	300
DK 5	60B	LEOPARD MOTH	1934	75	115	150
DK 6	60B	VAUTOUR	1957	35	55	75
DK 7	60C	HENRIOT H 180T	1935	100	150	200
DK 8	60C	PERCIVAL GULL	1934	50	75	100
DK 9	60C	LOCKHEED SUPER "AIR FRANCE CONSTELLATION"	1956	125	180	250
DK 10	60D	BREGUET "CORSAIRE"	1935	100	150	200
DK 11	60D	LOW WING MONOPLANE	1934	110	165	225
DK 12	60D	SIKORSKY S58 HELICOPTER	1957	50	75	100
DK 13	60E	DEWOITINE 500	1935	100	150	200
DK 14	60E	GENERAL MONOSPAR	1934	125	180	250
DK 15	60E	VICKERS VISCOUNT "AIR FRANCE"	1957	75	115	150
DK 16	60F	CIERVA AUTOGIRO (LARGE)	1935	165	220	375
DK 17	60F	CIERVA AUTOGIRO (SMALL)	1934	150	225	300
DK 18	60F	SE 210 CARAVELLE "AIR FRANCE"	1959	100	150	200
DK 19	60G	DEHAVILLAND COMET	1935-1946	75	115	150
DK 20	60H	SINGAPORE FLYING BOAT	1936	150	225	300
DK 21	60K	PERCIVAL GULL "LIGHT TOURER"	1946	50	75	100
DK 22	60M	FOUR ENGINE BOAT (SAME AS 60H) FLYING	1936	200	300	400
DK 23A	60N	FAIREY BATTLE BOMBER	1937	50	75	100
DK 23B	60P	GLOSTER GLADIATOR	1937	75	115	150
DK 24	60R	EMPIRE FLYING BOAT	1937-1946	55	80	110
DK 25	60S	CAMO MED BOMBER (SAME AS 60N-G)	1938	50	75	100
DK 26	60T	DOUGLAS DC-3	1938	185	265	350
DK 27	60V	ARMSTRONG WHITLEY BOMBER	1937	100	150	200
DK 28	60W	CLIPPER III FLYING BOAT	1938-1940	100	150	200
DK 29	60X	ATLANTIC FLYING BOAT (SAME AS 60R)	1937	350	575	700
DK 30	61A	DEWOITINE D 338 (SAME AS 30A)	1938	150	225	300
DK 31	61B	POTEZ 56	1938	100	150	200
DK 32	61C	FARMAN F360	1938	100	150	200
DK 33	61D	POTEZ 58	1938	100	150	200
DK 34	60E	HENRIOT H 180 M	1938	100	150	200
DK 35	61F	DEWOITINE CHASSEUR	1938	110	165	225
DK 36	62A	SUPERMARINE SPITFIRE	1940-1946	45	65	90
DK 37	62B	BRISTOL BLENHEIM (MEDIUM BOMBER)	1940-1946	25	35	50
DK 38	62D	CAMOUFLAGED BLENHEIM	1940	75	115	150

	MAN#	DESCRIPTION	YR. OF MAN.	C6	C8	C10
DK 39	62E	CAMOUFLAGED SPITFIRE	1940	85	130	175
DK 40	62G	BOEING FLYING FORTRESS	1939-1946	110	165	225
DK 41	62H	CAMOUFLAGED HURRICANE WITH OR WITHOUT WHEELS	1939	85	130	175
DK 42	62K	THE KINGS AIRSPEED ENVOY	1938	150	225	300
DK 43	62M	AIRSPEED ENVOY	1938-1946	125	185	250
DK 44	62N	JUNKER JU-90	1938	125	185	250
DK 45	62P	ARMSTRONG WHITWORTH ENSIGN	1938-1945	70	105	140
DK 46	62R	DE HAVILLAND ALBATROSS	1939-1946	60	90	120
DK 47	62S	HAWKER HURRICANE (SAME AS 62H)	1939-1946	30	45	60
DK 48	62T	CAMOUFLAGED WHITLEY BOMBER	1939	150	225	300
DK 49	62W	IMPERIAL AIRWAYS FROBISHER AIRLINER	1939	200	300	400
DK 50	62X	BRITISH 40 SEATER AIRLINER	1939	125	185	250
DK 51	62Y	GIANT HIGH SPEED MONOPLANE JU-90	1939-1946	175	265	350
DK 52	63A	MAIA FLYING BOAT	1939	200	300	400
DK 53	63B	MERCURY SEAPLANE	1939 & 1946	35	55	75
DK 54	64A	AMIOT 370	1939 & 1946	125	185	250
DK 55	64B	BLOCH	1939 & 1946	125	185	250
DK 56	64C	POTEZ 63	1939 & 1946	150	225	300
DK 57	64D	POTEZ 662	1939 & 1946	150	225	300
DK 58	66A	HEAVY BOMBER (SAME AS 60A)	1940	250	375	500
DK 59	66B	DIVEBOMBER (SAME AS 60B)	1940	250	375	500
DK 60	66C	TWO SEATER FIGHTER (SAME AS 60C)	1940	250	375	500
DK 61	66D	TORPEDO DIVE BOMBER (SAME AS 60A)	1940	250	375	500
DK 62	66E	MEDIUM BOMBER (SAME AS 60C)	1940	250	375	500
DK 63	66F	ARMY CO-OPERATION AUTOGIRO (SAME AS 60F)	1940	250	375	500
DK 64	67A	JUNKER JU-80 BOMBER (SAME AS 62N)	1940	200	300	400
DK 65	68A	ARMSTRONG WHITWORTH (SAME AS 62P)	1940	70	105	140
DK 66	68B	FROBISHER LINER (SAME AS 62R)	1940	60	90	120
DK 67	70A	AVRO YORK AIRLINER (SAME AS # 704)	1946	35	50	70
DK 68	70B	HAWKER TEMPEST II FIGHTER (# 730)	1946	35	50	75
DK 69	70R	VICKERS VIKING AIRLINER (# 705)	1947	20	30	40
DK 70	70D	TWIN ENGINE FIGHTER (# 731)	1946	25	38	50
DK 71	70E	GLOSTER METEOR FIGHTER (# 732)	1946	25	38	50
DK 72	70F	LOCKHEED SHOOTING STAR (# 733)	1947	20	30	40
DK 73 A	A700	RAF SPITFIRE DIAMOND JUBILEE SPITFIRE	1979	125	185	250
DK 73 B	B700	SEAPLANE (SAME AS 63B)	1954	35	50	75
DK 73 C	C701	SHETLAND FLYING BOAT	1947	300	450	600
DK 74	702	DH COMET JET AIRLINER "BOAC" (# 999)	1954	50	75	100
DK 75	704	AVRO YORK AIRLINER (# 70A)	1954	65	95	125
DK 76	705	VICKERS VIKING AIRLINER (# 70C)	1954	25	35	50
DK 77	706	VICKERS VISCOUNT AIRLINER "AIR FRANCE"	1956	45	60	90
DK 78	708	VICKERS VISCOUNT AIRLINER B.E.A.	1956	30	45	60
DK 79	710	BEECHCRAFT BONANZA	1965	30	45	60
DK 80	712	US ARMY T42A	1972	40	60	80
DK 81	715	BRISTOL 173 HELICOPTER	1956	30	45	60
DK 82	715	BEECHCRAFT C65 BARON	1968	30	45	60
DK 83	716	WESTLAND SIKORSKY S-51 HELICOPTER	1957	15	23	35

	MAN#	DESCRIPTION	YR. OF MAN.	C6	C8	C10
DK 84	717	BOEING 737 LUFTHANSA	1970	50	75	100
DK 85	718	HAWKER HURRICANE MKIIC	1972	80	110	150
DK 86	719	SUPERMARINE SPITFIRE MKII	1969	60	90	125
DK 87	721	JUNKERS JU87B STUKA	1969	40	60	100
DK 88	722	HAWKER HARRIER	1970	35	55	75
DK 89	723	HS 125 EXECUTIVE JET	1970	35	55	75
DK 90	724	SIKORSKY SEA KING HELICOPTER	1971	35	55	75
DK 91	725	F4K PHANTOM II "ROYAL NAVY"	1972	50	75	100
DK 92	726	MESSERSCHMITT 109E	1972	75	110	150
DK 93	727	F4 MARK II PHANTOM "US AIRFORCE"	1974	85	130	175
DK 94	728	R.A.F. DOMINIE	1972	30	45	60
DK 95	729	PANAVIA M.R.C.A. TORNADO	1973	35	55	75
DK 96	730	TEMPEST II FIGHTER (# 70B)	1954	15	25	35
DK 97	731	TWIN ENGINE FIGHTER (# 70D)	1954	10	18	25
DK 98	731	S.E.P.E.C.A.T. JAGUAR	1973	35	55	75
DK 99	732	GLOSTER METEOR TWIN JET FIGHTER (# 70E)	1954	15	20	30
DK 100	732	BELL 47 POLICE HELICOPTER	1972	35	55	75
DK 101	733	SHOOTINGSTAR JET (# 70F)	1954	20	30	40
DK 102	733	F4K PHANTOM II "BUNDESLUFTWAFFE	1973	75	115	150
DK 103	734	SUPERMARINE SWIFT FIGHTER	1955	15	22	30
DK 104	734	P47 THUNDERBOLT	1975	100	150	200
DK 105	735	GLOSTER JAVELIN FIGHTER	1956	20	30	45
DK 106	736	HAWKER HUNTER FIGHTER	1955	15	22	30
DK 107	736	BUNDESMARINE SEAKING HELICOPTER	1973	50	75	100
DK 108	737	B.A.C. LIGHTNING FIGHTER	1959	15	26	35
DK 109	738	DH 110 SEA VIXEN	1960	30	45	65
DK 110	739	JAPANESE A6M5 ZERO	1976	85	130	175
DK 111	741	SPITFIRE MARK II	1976	60	90	125
DK 112	744	SEA KING ARMY HELICOPTER	1976	40	55	75
DK 113	745	BELL 47 ARMY HELICOPTER	1978	40	55	75
DK 114	749	AVRO VULCAN BOMBER (992)	1955	1000	1500	2000
DK 115	800	MYSTERE IV-A FIGHTER	1959	40	55	75
DK 116	801	VAUTOUR FIGHTER	1959	40	55	75
DK 117	802	SIKORSKY S58 HELICOPTER	1959	50	75	100
DK 118	803	VICKERS VISCOUNT "AIR FRANCE"	1959	150	225	300
DK 119	804	NORD 2501 NORATLAS	1959	150	225	300
DK 120	891	SE 210 CARAVELLE FRENCH AIR FRANCE	1959	100	150	200
DK 121	892	LOCKHEED CONSTELLATION AIR FRANCE (60C)	1959	125	185	250
DK 122	997	SE 210 CARAVELLE BRITISH "AIR FRANCE"	1962	100	150	200
DK 123	998	BRISTOL BRITANNIA "CANADIAN PACIFIC"	1959	150	225	300
DK 124	999	DEHAVILLAND COMET	1956	50	75	100
DK 125	730	F-4 PHANTOM II US NAVY	1973	75	115	150
DKS-1		60 SETS of 6 PLANES PREWAR	—	—	—	3500

DK 5

DK 8

DK 11

DK 17

DK 19

20

A2113
DINKY TOYS No. 60h
SINGAPORE FLYING BOAT

DK 20

DK 23 - A

DK 27

DK 24

DK 28

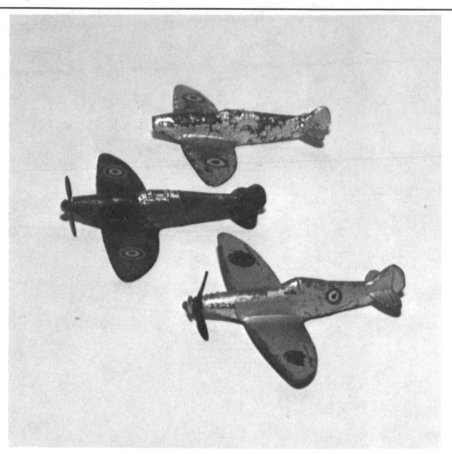

TOP TO BOTTOM: DK 36, DK 39, DK 36

DK 37

DK 40

DK 42

TOP TO BOTTOM: DK 41, DK 47, DK 41

DK 43

DK 48

DK 53

DK 66

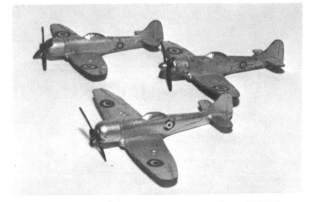

TOP: DK 68   BOTTOM: DK 96

DK 69

DK 70

DK 71
DK 71
DK 99

DK 72

Diamond Jubilee of the Royal Air Force

DK 73 - A

DK 78

DK 77

DK 75

DK 81

DK 83

DK 85

DK 86

26

DK 87

DK 88

CONDITION OF A TOY AND ITS RELATION TO PRICE
CONDITION CODE:

C6 - Good. Evident overall wear, well-played with, but acceptable to many collectors.

C8 - Very Good Minor wear overall, very clean.

C10 - Mint (like new).

Note: Mint in Box commands a higher price. Condition below C6 brings considerably lower prices.

DK 91

DK 92

DK 92

DK 92

DK 94

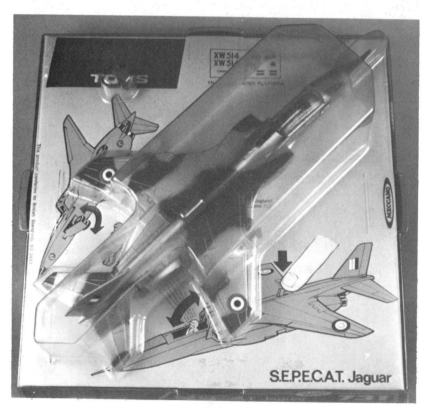

DK 98

DK 103

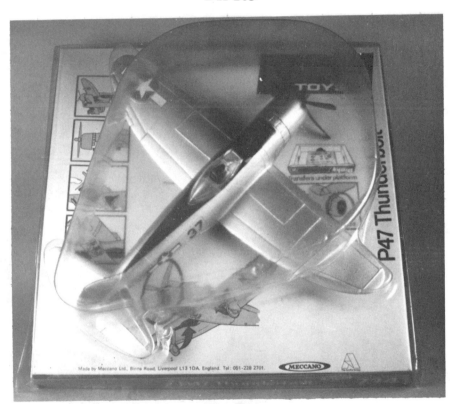

DK 104

DK 105

DK 106

DK 108

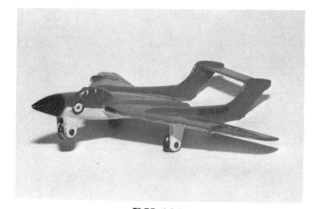

DK 109

DK 110

DK 114

DK 115

DK 116

DK 117

DK 119

DK 120

DK 121

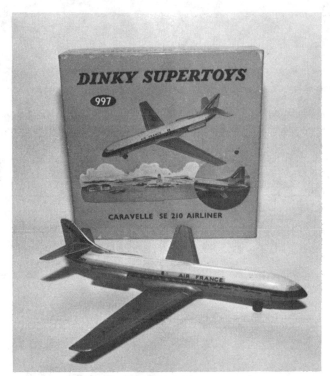

DK 122

DK 123

DK 124

DK 125

CONDITION OF A TOY AND ITS RELATION TO PRICE
CONDITION CODE:

C6 - Good. Evident overall wear, well-played with, but acceptable to many collectors.

C8 - Very Good Minor wear overall, very clean.

C10 - Mint (like new).

Note: Mint in Box commands a higher price. Condition below C6 brings considerably lower prices.

EDISON
Italian Die Cast

	MAN #	DESCRIPTION	C6	C8	C10
ED 1	1001	R.A.F. S.E.5a BIPLANE	40	60	80
ED 2	1002	FOKKER DR-1 TRIPLANE (RED BARON)	50	70	90
ED 3	1003	SPAD S XIII BIPLANE	40	60	80
ED 4	1004	MACCHI NIEUPORT BIPLANE	40	60	80
ED 5	1101	ANSALDO A I "BALILLA" BIPLANE	40	60	80
ED 6	1102	AVIATIK D1 "BERG" BIPLANE	40	60	80
ED 7	1103	ANSALDO SOPWITH "BABY" BIPLANE W/FLOATS	50	70	90
ED 8	1104	HANSA-BRANDENBURG D1 BIPLANE	40	60	80
ED 9	1201	SUPERMARINE S5 LOWWING RACER W/FLOATS	75	100	150
ED 10	1202	MACCHI CASTOLDI MC72 LOWWING RACER W/FLOATS	75	100	150
ED 11	1203	GEEBEE SUPER SPORTSTER	100	150	200
ED 12	1204	GRUMMAN "GULF HAWK" (NOT ISSUED)	N. P. F.		

(N.P.F. - NO PRICE FOUND)

ED 1

37

ED 2

ED 3

ED 4

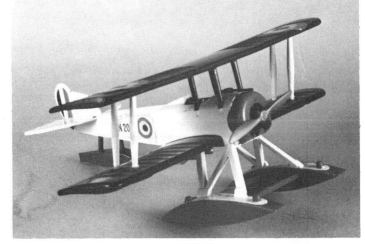

ED 7

ED 5

ED 8

ED 6

ED 9

ED 10

ED 11

ERIE
Die Cast

MAN #		DESCRIPTION	C6	C8	C10
ER 1	—	NORTHROP GAMA LARGE 2 PC CASTING	100	150	200
ER 2	—	NORTHROP GAMA SMALL 1 PC CASTING	35	55	75
ER 3	—	NORTHROP DELTA PASSENGER LARGE	75	115	150
ER 4	—	BOEING B-17 LARGE 2 PC CASTING	65	95	125
ER 5	—	BOEING 247 SMALL 1 PC CASTING	25	35	50

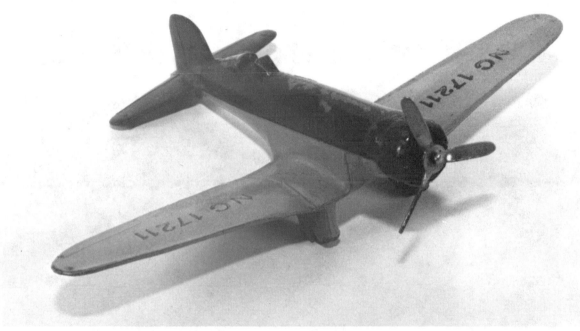

ER 1

ER 3

ER 4

ER 5

ER 2

CONDITION OF A TOY AND ITS RELATION TO PRICE
CONDITION CODE:

C6 — Good. Evident overall wear, well-played with, but acceptable to many collectors.

C8 — Very Good Minor wear overall, very clean.

C10 — Mint (like new).

Note: Mint in Box commands a higher price. Condition below C6 brings considerably lower prices.

FASTWING PLAY ART
Die Cast 1978

MAN #	TYPE	C6	C8	C10
FW 1	7400	IL-2M3 STORMOVIC	10	20	30
FW 2	7401	AW SEAHAWK	10	20	30
FW 3	7402	JET PROVOST T MK 3	10	20	30
FW 4	7403	FAIREY BATTLE	10	20	30
FW 5	7404	NA P5IB MUSTANG	10	20	30
FW 6	7405	JUNKER JU 87 B	10	20	30
FW 7	7406	LOCKHEED LIGHTNING P-38	10	20	30
FW 8	7407	CHANCE VOUGHT F4U ID CORSAIR	10	20	30
FW 9	7408	ME 110 D	10	20	30
FW 10	7409	HURRICANE IV	10	20	30
FW 11	7410	MESSERSCHMITT ME-410	10	20	30
FW 12	7411	GRUMMAN WILDCAT VI	10	20	30
FW 13	7412	NA	—	—	—
FW 14	7413	GRUMMAN F6F-5 HELLCAT	10	20	30
FW 15	7414	NA	—	—	—
FW 16	7415	NA	—	—	—
FW 17	7416	SUPERMARINE SPITFIRE MKII	10	20	30
FW 18	7417	MITSUBISHI TYPE ZERO	10	20	30
FW 19	7418	HENSCHEL HS 123	10	20	30
FW 20	7419	FIAT CR 42 BIPLANE	20	30	40
FW 21	7420	NA	—	—	—
FW 22	7421	NA	—	—	—
FW 23	7422	BOEING CLIPPER	10	20	30
FW 24	7423	NA	—	—	—

FW 1

FW 2

FW 3

FW 5

FW 6

FW 7

FW 8　　　　　　　　　　　　**FW 9**

FW 10　　　　　　　　　　　　**FW 12**

FW 14

FW 17

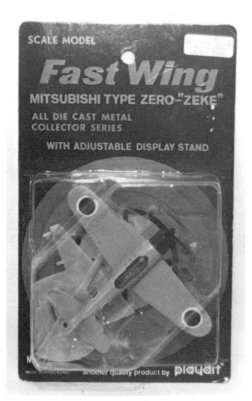

FW 18

FW 19

FW 20   **FW 23**

CONDITION CODE:

C6 - Good. Evident overall wear, well played
with, but acceptable to many collectors

C8 - Very Good Minor wear overall, very clean

C10 - Mint (like new)

Note: Mint in Box commands a higher price. Condition below C6 brings considerable lower prices.

HUBLEY
Die Cast

TYPE		C6	C8	C10
HU 1	BELL AIRACUDA XFM-1	100	200	350
HU 2	U.S. ARMY PLANE #431	40	75	100
HU 3	JET FOLDING WINGS #430	30	40	60
HU 4	TWIN ENGINE TWIN VERT. STABILIZER 3B4	30	40	60
HU 5	U.S. ARMY LOW WING PROP FOLDING WHEELS	40	60	85
HU 6	P-39 CAST WITH TIN WING SOLID COCKPIT	10	20	30
HU 7	AMERICAN EAGLE/FLYING CIRCUS FOLDING WINGS #495	50	75	100
HU 8	PIPER CUB L4, RED OR OLIVE #433	20	50	75
HU 9	P-40 EARLY VER. 3 BLADE, NEWER 2 BLADE	15	30	50
HU 10	P-38 FOLDING LANDING GEAR	50	90	150
	(RED-SILVER) (YELLOW-GREEN) (CAMO)			
HU 11	BREWSTER BUFFALO #467	20	40	60
HU 12	DELTA WING JET-FOLDING WING AND GEAR #751	20	30	40
HU 13	CRUSADER TWIN BOOM #427	20	40	60

HU 1

HU 2

HU 7

HU 8

HU 9

HU 9

HU 10

HU 10

HU 11

HU 13

LINTOY
Die Cast

	TYPE	C6	C8	C10
LT 1	DOUGLAS A20 BOSTON/HAVOC	10	15	25
LT 2	GRUMMAN F-11A TIGER #11	10	20	35
LT 3	MESSERSCHMITT ME262	10	20	35
LT 4	MESSERSCHMITT ME-410	10	20	35
LT 5	MIG-21 #08	10	25	40
LT 6	NA-P-51D	10	25	40
LT 7	SAAB 35X DRAKEN #07	10	20	35
LT 8	SEPECAT JAGUAR #10	10	20	35

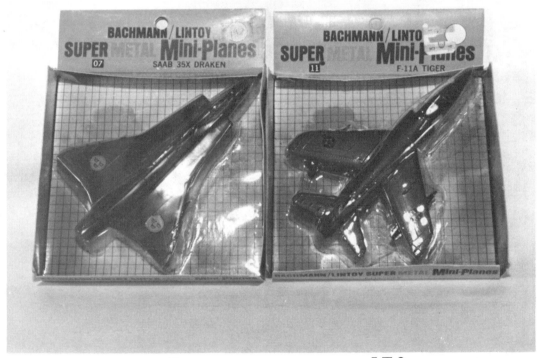

LT 7   LT 2

CONDITION OF A TOY AND ITS RELATION TO PRICE
CONDITION CODE:

C6 - Good. Evident overall wear, well-played with, but acceptable to many collectors.

C8 - Very Good Minor wear overall, very clean.

C10 - Mint (like new).

Note: Mint in Box commands a higher price. Condition below C6 brings considerably lower prices.

LT 6

LT 3   **LT 4**

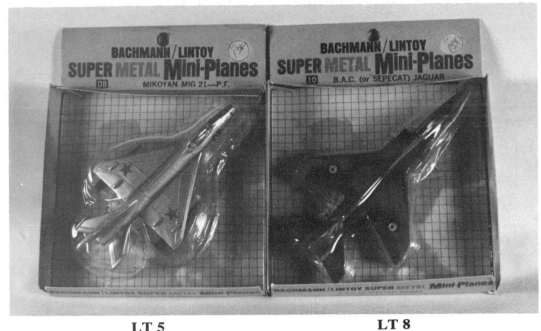

LT 5   LT 8

MERCURY AIRCRAFT
Italy

From the Martin Braunlich Collection

(N.P.F. - NO PRICE FOUND)

	MAN #	TYPE	C6	C8	C10
MR 1	400A	SCATOLA 8 PLANE GIFT SET	N. P. F.		
MR 2	400B	SCATOLA 8 PLANE GIFT SET	N. P. F.		
MR 3	400C	SCATOLA 14 PLANE GIFT SET	N. P. F.		
MR 4	401	FIAT G-59	75	110	150
MR 5	402	FIAT G-212	50	75	100
MR 6	402A	FIAT G-212 RED CROSS	75	110	150
MR 7	403	FIAT G-80	40	60	85
MR 8	404	VAMPIRE	40	60	85
MR 9	405	LOCKHEED F-90	40	60	85
MR 10	406	AVRO 707A	40	60	85
MR 11	407	COMET DH 106	75	110	150
MR 12	408	DASSAULT MYSTERE	25	35	50
MR 13	409	MISSILE	65	95	125
MR 14	410	NORTH AMERICAN F-86 SABRE	40	60	85
MR 15	411	PIAGGIO P-148	50	75	100
MR 16	412	MIG-15	25	35	50
MR 17	413	CONVAIR XF-92A	25	35	50
MR 18	414	PIAGGIO P-136	75	110	150
MR 19	415	BOEING B-50	75	110	150
MR 20	416	CONVAIR B-36E	125	175	250
MR 21	417	SIKORSKY S-55	40	60	75
MR 22	418	BOEING B-47 STRATOJET	50	75	100
MR 23	419	DOUGLAS D 558-2 SKYROCKET	100	150	200
MR 24	420	MIG 19	25	35	50
MR 25	421	CONVAIR XFY-1 POGO	100	175	200
MR 26	422	CUTLASS F7U-3	35	55	75
MR 27	423	CORSAIR F4U-5N	100	150	200
MR 28	424	LOCKHEED F-94C STARFIRE	50	75	100
MR 29	425	LOCKHEED P-38 LIGHTNING	90	135	185
MR 30	426	REPUBLIC XF-91	150	225	300

MR 5

MR 9

MR 10

MR 7

MR 11

MR 8

MR 12

MR 14

MR 18

MR 15

MR 19

MR 16

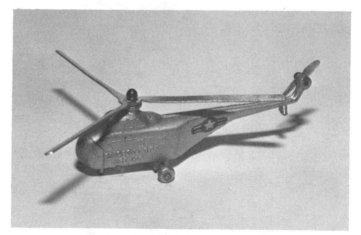

MR 21

MR 17

MR 20

MR 22

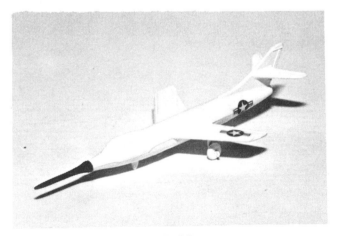

MR 23

MR 24

MR 26

MR 25

MR 29

SOLIDO

Started production in 1934 from a manufacturing plant just outside Paris. From 1955 to 1963 produced its finest diecast aircraft. *All photos Braunlich Collection.*

(N.P.F. - NO PRICE FOUND)

	MAN #	TYPE	C6	C8	C10
SL 1	026A	AVION "ANPHIBIE" BUILDS PLANE/CAR/BOAT	N. P. F.		
SL 2	036	AVION I BUILDS 6 MODELS	N. P. F.		
SL 3	142	AVION II BUILDS 12 MODELS	N. P. F.		
SL 4	145	AVION III BUILDS 18 MODELS	N. P. F.		
SL 5	145A	AVION IV BUILDS 25 MODELS	N. P. F.		
SL 6	146A	AVION V SHOOTING STAR STRAIGHT WINGS	40	55	75
SL 7	146B	AVION V SHOOTING STAR SWEPT BACK WINGS	30	45	60
SL 8	163	MYSTERE IV	20	30	40
SL 9	164	FOUGA MAGISTER W/O WING TIP TANKS	20	30	40
SL 10	164	FOUGA MAGISTER W/WING TIP TANKS	40	60	80
SL 11	165	SKYRAY "US STAR"	20	30	40
SL 12	165	SKYRAY "US STAR & NAVY"	35	55	75
SL 13	166	VAUTOUR	35	50	70
SL 14	167	LEDUC 021 IN SILVER	20	30	40
SL 15	167	LEDUC 021 IN GREEN	50	75	100
SL 16	168	SUPER SABRE F-100 "US STAR"	20	30	40
SL 17	168	SUPER SABRE F-100 "US STAR & USAF"	30	45	60
SL 18	169	SIKORSKY S-55	35	50	70
SL 19	169	SIKORSKY S-55 "RED CROSS"	40	60	80
SL 20	170	MIG-15	20	60	40
SL 21	171	HAWKER HUNTER	20	30	45
SL 22	172	THUNDERJET	40	55	75
SL 23	173	BAROUDEUR	N.P.F.		
SL 24	174	JAVELIN	30	45	60
SL 25	175	SUPER CONSTELLATION "TWA"	100	150	200
SL 26	176	CARAVELLE "AIRFRANCE"	45	60	90
SL 27	176-01	CARAVELLE "FINNAIR"	N.P.F.		
SL 28	176-02	CARAVELLE "ALITALIA"	N.P.F.		
SL 29	176-03	CARAVELLE "AIR MAROC"	N.P.F.		
SL 30	176-06	CARAVELLE "SUD AVIATION"	N.P.F.		
SL 31	176-08	CARAVELLE "VARIG"	N.P.F.		
SL 32	176-13	CARAVELLE "SWISS AIR"	N.P.F.		
SL 33	176-14	CARAVELLE "UNITED"	N.P.F.		
SL 34	176-15	CARAVELLE "AIR ALGERIE"	N.P.F.		
SL 35	176-16	CARAVELLE "SAS"	N.P.F.		
SL 36	177	SUPER CIGALE	20	30	40
SL 37	178	TRIDENT	30	40	60
SL 38	179	FAIREY DELTA TYPE 2	N.P.F.		
SL 39	180	CONVAIR X.F.Y.1. "US STAR, USAF, USN	30	45	60
SL 40	181A	PIASECKI H-21 (BLUE OR SILVER WINDOWS)	90	135	180
SL 41	181B	VERTOL H-21 (BLUE OR SILVER WINDOWS)	100	150	200

	MAN #	TYPE		C6	C8	C10
SL 42	182	MORANE SAULNIER PARIS		20	30	40
SL 43	183	AQUILLON		30	45	60
SL 44	184	SUPER MYSTERE B-2		20	30	40
SL 45	185	ETENDARA IV			N.P.F.	
SL 46	186	BREGUET ALIZE			N.P.F.	
SL 47	187	TUPOLEV TU 104			N.P.F.	
SLBXS		SOLIDO OFFERED BOXED SETS BUT NO PHOTOS OR PRICES AVAILABLE				

(N.P.F. - NO PRICE FOUND)

SL 11

SL 22

SL 17

SL 40

TEKNO

Started in 1928 Tekno manufactured tin plate toys. Because of the war, tinplate production was banned from 1940 to 1952. During German occupation the owner was arrested for making diecast toy airplanes thought to be dangerous to the occupiers. He was released shortly but all airplane inventory was confiscated. A quality toy they are highly sought after by collectors today.

	MAN #	TYPE	C6	C8	C10
TK 1	401	FLYVENDE FAESTING B-17 TYPE VARIOUS MARKINGS	65	90	125
TK 2	401	FLYVENDE FAESTING B-17 TYPE W/ LUFTWAFFE MARKINGS	250	375	500
TK 3	402	BBI TWIN ENGINE VARIOUS MARKINGS "BLENHIEM"	35	50	75
TK 4	403	JAGER DBS 1 VARIOUS MARKINGS "DOUGLAS"	40	60	85
TK 5	488	TWIN ENGINE HOSPITAL PLANE VARIOUS MARKINGS	125	185	250
TK 6	488	TWIN ENGINE HOSPITAL PLANE W/"1939-1949" DECAL	250	375	500
TK 7	765	DC-7 "KLM/ALITALIA/SABENA/SAS/SUDFLUG/OR SWISS AIR"	125	185	250
TK 8	766	CARAVELLE SE 210 "AIRFRANCE/SAS/SWISS AIR"	125	185	250
TK 9	785	HAWKER HUNTER RAF JET	75	115	150
TK 10	786	MIG 15 JET	75	115	150
TK 11	787	SUPER SABRE F-100 "DANISH/US AIRFORCE"	90	125	175
TK 12	788	SUPER MYSTERE "DANISH/FRENCH"	90	125	175
TK 13	TKBS	BOXED SET THREE MODELS	—	—	300

NOTE: SEE TINPLATE SECTION FOR TEKNO TIN HOSPITAL PLANE

TK 1

TK 3

TK 4

TK 5

TK 5

TK 5

TK 7

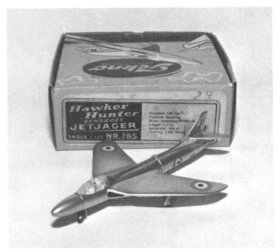

TK 9

TK 10

TK 11

TK 12

TK 13

TOOTSIETOY

This firm produced its first toy in 1906 and hasn't stopped yet. Although toys sold in the 1920 and 1960 period hold most collectors interest, you can still fined Tootsietoy product on the shelves of most major discount department stores as well as Toys-R-Us.

	MAN #	TYPE	C6	C8	C10
TT 1	1031	BUCK ROGERS "BATTLE CRUSER" (GROOVED WHEELS)	85	150	300
TT 2	1033	BUCK ROGERS "FLASH BLAST" (GROOVED WHEELS)	85	150	300
TT 3	1032	BUCK ROGERS "VENUS DUO DESTROYERS" (GROOVED WHEELS)	85	150	350
TT 4	1030	"USN LOS ANGELES" (GROOVED WHEELS)	85	150	260
TT 5	106	LOCKHEED SIRUS LOW WING	15	25	50
TT 6	107	BELLANCA HIGHWING	15	25	50
TT 7	119	NORTHROP "US ARMY"	10	15	25
TT 8	125	LOCKHEED ELECTRA TWIN ENGINE	10	15	20
TT 9	717	D C-2 "TWA"	20	35	50
TT 10	718	WACO BIPLANE "US NAVY"	60	75	100
TT 11	718	WACO BIPLANE "DIVE BOMBER"	90	125	150
TT 12	719	CRUSADER TWIN ENGINE	40	60	75
TT 13	720	AUTOGYRO SMALL VERSION "FLY-N-GYRO" (GROOVED WHEELS)	150	200	250
TT 14	721	CURTISS P-40	75	125	150
TT 15	722	DC4 "SUPERMAINLINER"	20	40	50
TT 16	722	DC4 MILITARY "ARMY TRANSPORT"	40	60	75
TT 17	4482	BLEROIT (LARGER VERSION)	40	50	60
TT 18	4491	BLERIOT (SMALLER VERSION)	25	40	50
TT 19	4649	FORD TRIMOTOR	60	100	125
TT 20	4650	BIPLANE	40	60	75
TT 21	4659	AUTOGYRO LARGE VERSION W/TIN WING	75	100	125
TT 22	4660	AERO-DAWN "UX-214"	20	40	50
TT 23	4660	AERO DAWN FLOAT PLANE "UX-214"	30	50	60
TT 24	4675	BIPLANE TIN WINGS	20	30	40
TT 25	4675	BIPLANE TIN WINGS FLOATPLANE	30	40	50
TT 26	xxxx	P-38 TWIN ENGINE TWIN BOOM	30	60	75
TT 27	xxxx	P-39 SINGLE ENGINE TIN-LITHO-WING-2 BLADE PROP	50	70	90
TT 28	xxxx	LOCKHEED CONSTELLATION "PAA N88846"	40	60	80
TT 29	xxxx	BOEING 377 STRATOCRUISER "PAA N102SV"	40	60	80
TT 30	xxxx	PIPER CUB	5	10	15
TT 31	xxxx	NAVION	5	10	15
TT 32	xxxx	BEECHCRAFT BONANZA	5	10	15
TT32A	xxxx	F4D DOUGLAS SKYRAY	5	10	15
TT 33	xxxx	P-80 SHOOTING STAR JET	10	15	20
TT 34	xxxx	F7 U-3 CUTLASS JET	10	15	20
TT 35	xxxx	F 86 SABRE JET 2 PC CASTING	10	20	25
TT 36	xxxx	F 86 SABRE JET 1 PC CASTING	5	10	15
TT 37	xxxx	F9F-2 PANTHER JET 2 PC CASTING	10	20	25
TT 38		F9F-2 PANTHER JET 1 PC CASTING	5	10	15
TT 39		DELTA JET 2 PC CASTING	10	20	25
TT 40		F-94 STARFIRE JET	10	15	20

MAN #	TYPE		C6	C8	C10
TT 41		BOEING 707	10	15	20
TT 42		SIKORSKY S:43 "COASTGUARD" 2 ENGINE	60	80	150
TT 43		F4U CORSAIR (1988) DIECAST/PLASTIC	5	10	15
TT 44	2917	P-40 Curtiss (1988) DIECAST/PLASTIC	5	10	15
TT 45	2925	ZERO (1989)	x	x	1
TT 46	2925	STUKA (1989)	x	x	1
TT 47	2925	P-40 (1989)	x	x	1
TT 48	2925	F-4U CORSAIR (1989)	x	x	1
TT 49	2925	SPITFIRE (1989)	x	x	1
TT 50	2925	P-51 (1989)	x	x	1
TT 51	2925	B-17 BOMBER (1989)	x	x	2
TT 52	3260	THE REDBARON (1978)	50	75	100
TT 53		CONVAIR CV-240	20	30	45

TT 5

TT 8

TT 6

TT 9

TT 7

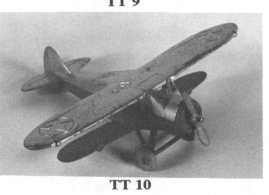

TT 10

TT 11

TT 11

TT 12

TT 13

TT 14

TT 15

TT 19

TT 21

TT 22

TT 22

TT 23

TT 27

TT 24

TT 31

TT 26

TT 42

TT 52

TT 53

MAN #	TYPE	C6	C8	C10
TTBXS 1	BOXED SET OF 5 AIRPLANES	x	x	600
TTBXS 2	BOXED AIRPORT SET	x	x	600
TTBXS 3	BOXED SET OF 11 AIRPLANES	x	x	1100

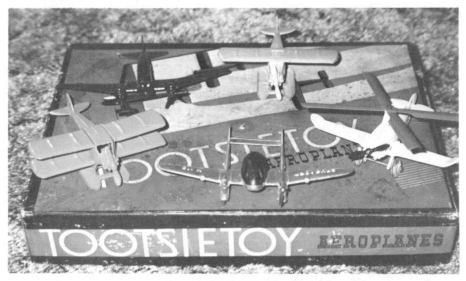

TTBXS 1

TTBXS 2

TTBXS 3

COLLECTION RICH SAVAGE

WILDWINGS/CRAGSTON

Die Cast Assorted Scales

	TYPE	C6	C8	C10
	1120—WWI SERIES			
WW 1	Spad XIII	10	20	30
WW 2	SE 5 Scout	10	20	30
WW 3	Sopwith Camel	10	20	30
WW 4	Fokker D7	10	20	30
	1121—WWII SERIES			
WW 5	P-51 Mustang	10	20	30
WW 6	Japanese Zero	10	20	30
WW 7	British Spitfire	10	20	30
WW 8	ME 109 Messerschmitt	10	20	30
	1122—US JET SERIES			
WW 9	F105 THUNDERCHIEF	10	20	30
WW 10	F111 SWINGWING	10	20	30
WW 11	F86 SABERJET	10	20	30
WW 12	F104 STARFIGHTER	10	20	30
	1123—AIRPLANE JET SERIES			
WW 13	BOEING 707	10	20	30
WW 14	BRITISH VC-10	10	20	30
WW 15	BOEING 727 WHISPER	10	20	30
	1124—HELICOPTER SERIES			
WW 16	PIASEKI WORKHORSE	15	25	35
WW 17	HUEY COBRA	15	25	35
WW 18	PIASEKI TWIN JET	15	25	35
WW 19	SIKORSKY HO4S	15	25	35

WILDWING/CRAGSTON

		C6	C8	C10
	1125—SERIES N/A			
	1126—SERIES N/A			
	1127—HISTORIC SERIES			
WW 20	SPIRIT OF ST LOUIS	15	25	35
WW 21	FORD TRI MOTOR	15	25	35
WW 22	PBY CATALINA	15	25	35
WW 23	DOUGLAS DC-3	15	25	35
	1128—PRIVATE PLANE SERIES			
WW 24	BEECHCRAFT SUPER 18	10	20	30
WW 25	CESSNA 180	10	20	30
WW 26	LEAR JET	10	20	30
WW 27	CESSNA T-37	10	20	30
	1129—INTERNATIONAL SERIES			
WW 28	RUSSIAN MIG-21	15	25	35
WW 29	FRENCH MYSTERE B2	15	25	35
WW 30	BRITISH BUCCANEER	15	25	35
WW 31	ISRAELI MIRAGE III R	15	25	35

WW 1

WW 2

WW 3

WW 4

WW 5

WW 6

WW 7

WW 8

WW 9

WW 10

WW 11

WW 12

WW 13

WW 14

WW 15

WW 16

WW 17

WW 18

WW 19

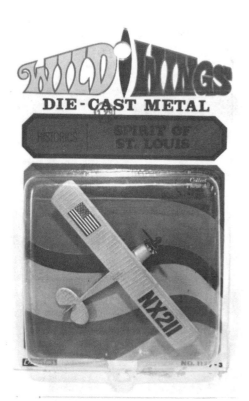

WW 20

WW 21

WW 23

WW 24

WW 25

WW 26

WW 27

WW 28

WW 29

WW 30

WW 31

**CONDITION OF A TOY AND ITS RELATION TO PRICE
CONDITION CODE:**

C6 - Good. Evident overall wear, well-played with, but acceptable to many collectors.

C8 - Very Good Minor wear overall, very clean.

C10 - Mint (like new).

Note: Mint in Box commands a higher price. Condition below C6 brings considerably lower prices.

MISCELLANEOUS AIRCRAFT

	MAN #	TYPE	C6	C8	C10
LS 1		LONESTAR VICKERS VICOUNT	50	75	100
LS 2		LONESTAR DE HAVILLAND COMET	100	150	200
LS 3		LONESTAR BOEING PAN AM 707	100	150	200
CIJ-1		CIJ 707 "AIRFRANCE"	20	30	40
CIJ-2		CIJ CARAVELLE "AIRFRANCE"	20	30	40
SW-1		SUPERWING F-15 EAGLE	75	110	150
MA-1		MINI AIR CONCORD	50	75	100
MA-2		MINI AIR 747 PAN AM	65	95	125
MA-3		MINI AIR 747 JAPAN AIRLINES	75	110	150
EK-1		EKO F86F PLASTIC	10	15	20
EK-2		EKO F84 F PLASTIC	10	15	20
EK-3		EKO HAWKER HURRICANE PLASTIC	10	15	20
EK-4		EKO MITSUBISHI ZERO PLASTIC	10	15	20
POL-1		POLITOY F-105 THUNDERCHIEF	10	15	25
POL-2		POLITOY FIAT G-91	10	15	25
CR 1		CR DEPERDUSSIOUN	45	65	90
RB-1		STEARMAN REDBARON PIZZA BIPLANE PROMO	10	15	25
CC-1		STEARMAN CADBURY CRUNCHIE BIPLANE PROMO	20	30	40
VA-1		PITTS BIPLANE VIRGIN ATLANTIC	10	15	20
MA-1		DC-3 MADE IN ARGENTINA	25	35	50
MA-2		LOCKHEED ELECTRA MADE IN ARGENTINA	25	35	50
KC-1	113-1	MUSTANG P51 D "MISS DETROIT"	20	30	40
KC-2	113-2	F4U-4 CORSAIR	15	22	30
KC-3	113-3	P.40B TIGER SHARK	15	22	30
KC-4	113-4	SPITFIRE	15	22	30
KC-5	113-5	MITSUBISHI ZERO	15	22	30
KC-6	113-6	STUKA JU87 Gl	15	22	30
RN-1		TWA LOCKHEED CONSTELLATION	75	125	200

LS 1

LS 2

LS 3

CIJ 1

CIJ 2

SW 1

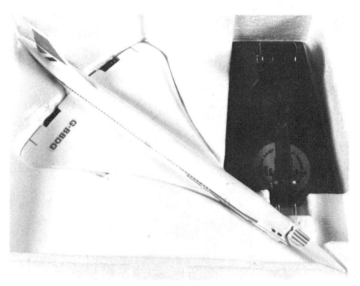

MA 1

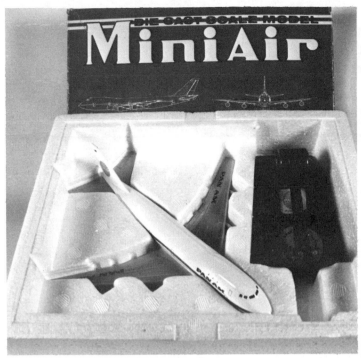

MA 2

MA 3

EK 1

EK 2

POL 1

CR 1

RB 1

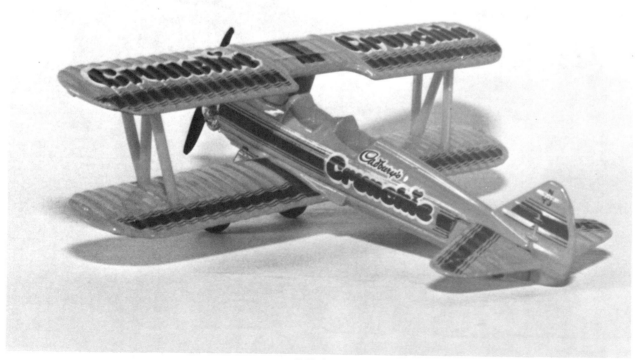

CC 1

88

VA 1

MA 1

MA 2

CONDITION OF A TOY AND ITS RELATION TO PRICE
CONDITION CODE:

C6 - Good. Evident overall wear, well-played with, but acceptable to many collectors.

C8 - Very Good Minor wear overall, very clean.

C10 - Mint (like new).

Note: Mint in Box commands a higher price. Condition below C6 brings considerably lower prices.

KC 1

KC 2

KC 3

KC 4

KC 5

KC 6

TIN AIRCRAFT

	TYPE	MAN.	POWER	WINGSPAN	C6	C8	C10
T 1	ALL NIPPON AIRWAYS TRISTAR	JAPAN	B / O	—	150	250	300
T 2	ALL NIPPON AIRWAYS TRISTAR	JAPAN	F	—	100	150	200
T 3	AIR FRANCE	?	R / C	—	125	175	250
T 4	AIRFRANCE SUPER G CONSTELLATION	JOUSTRA	F	19½″	225	300	450
T 5	AMERICAN AIRLINES DC7 STRATOCRUISER	?	F	—	100	125	175
T 6	AMERICAN AIRLINES DC-7C	JAPAN	B / O	24″	300	475	650
T 7	AMERICAN AIRLINES AA-100	JAPAN	F	—	150	250	375
T 8	AMERICAN AIRLINES ELECTRA	LINEMAR	B / O	20″	250	375	500
T 9	AMERICAN AIRLINES BOEING 727	Y	B / O	16″	100	150	225
T 10	AMERICAN AIRLINES "PAMILA"	LINEMAR	F	15″	100	150	250
T 11	AEROMOBILE	W.GER	W / U	8″	40	90	175
T 12	AVION VOLTERETAS	RICO	W / U	4¾″	60	100	150
T 13	B-26 BOMBER	BANDAI	F	—	25	50	75
T 14	B-45 TORNADO NA	BANDAI	F	16″	100	150	250
T 15	B-50	BANDAI	F	7½″	40	60	90
T 16	B-36	Y	F	26″	300	600	900
T 17	B-29	Y	F	19″	150	300	475
T 18	B-47 USAF	DAIYA	F	12″	150	225	325
T 19	B-50	Y	B / O	19″	200	300	400
T 20	B-50	TCP	F	15″	200	300	400
T 21	B-50	JAPAN	F	15″	200	300	400
T 22	B-58 HUSTLER CONVAIR	MARX	B / O	19″	250	400	560
T 23	BEECHCRAFT BONANZA A 104	TM	B / O	—	100	150	200
T 24	BEECHCRAFT TWIN ENGINE	TM	R / C	—	90	125	175
T 25	BLACKNIGHT DOUGLAS F3H DEMON	JAPAN	—	—	125	200	275
T 26	BIPLANE (CONSTRUCTION)	JAPAN	F	—	150	200	300
T 27	BLUEBIRD SEAPLANE	S & E	F	13″	50	80	175
T 28	BLUEHEAVEN	JAPAN	W / U	—	75	100	150
T 29	BRISTOL BULLDOG	S & E	B / O	14½″	150	200	300
T 30	CAPITOL AIRLINES VICOUNT	JAPAN	R / C	—	90	125	175
T 31	CAPITOL AIRLINES VICKERS VICOUNT	JAPAN	B / O	—	125	190	275
T 32	CESSNA USAF-105	W / GER	F	12″	100	175	250
T 33	CESSNA	TN	F	25″	100	200	400
T 34	CESSNA N8958	JAPAN	B / O	—	60	80	120
T 34A	CESSNA-HWN-70	W.GER	ELEC	8⅛″	60	80	120
T 35	CESSNA A-37	JAPAN	F	—	60	80	120
T 35A	CESSNA TWIN PROP-FRONT—BACK	Y	F	11¼″	125	225	325
T 36	LAI CONSTELLATION	INGAP	W / U	15″	125	275	450
T 37	COMET 116 FLOAT PLANE	JAPAN	W / U	6″	150	200	275
T 38	COMET DH 106	TM	F	7″	40	60	100
T 39	COMET JET AIRLINER	JAPAN	F	—	40	60	100
T 40	CRAGSTON JET 38710	JAPAN	F	14½″	90	120	150
T 40A	CRAGSTON BIPLANE 7F18	TN	B / O	14¼″	250	325	400
T 41	CV-440 CONVAIR TIPPCO WORLD	TIPP	W / U	—	300	400	600
T 42	CLIPPER FLOAT PLANE	?	W / U	—	150	200	275
T 43	CLIPPER TWIN ENGINE FLOAT	JAPAN	W / U	—	150	225	300

TYPE		MAN.	POWER	WINGSPAN	C6	C8	C10
T 44	C-120 PACK PLANE	JAPAN	F	16"	500	700	900
T 45	C-124 MILITARY AIR TRANSPORT	Y	F	20"	500	700	900
T 46	C-124 MILITARY AIR TRANSPORT	Y	B / O	20"	600	700	900
T 47	C-124 TROOP CARRIER	JAPAN	F	20"	500	700	900
T 48	C-130 HERCULES LOCKHEED	JAPAN	—	—	400	600	800
T 49	C-141 STARLIFTER	JAPAN	B / O	—	200	300	400
T 50	COMET JETLINER	Y	F	19"	200	300	400
T 51	DEMON NAVY JET (BATT-LIGHTS)	TN	F	8½"	50	75	125
T 52	DOUGLAS TRIMOTOR	CK	W / U	10"	900	1300	1800
T 53	DOUGLAS TRIMOTOR (1937)	JAPAN	W / U	10"	900	1300	1800
T 54	D-558 GOLDEN ARROW SKYROCKET	JAPAN	F	—	150	225	300
T 55	DOUGLAS AIR WAY	JAPAN	—	—	200	300	400
T 56	DISNEY COMIC PLANE	LINEMAR	F	10"	200	300	400
T 57	DEHAVILLAND COMET	RICO	F	11½"	200	300	400
T 58	EASTERN CONSTELLATION	MSK	F	7½"	100	150	200
T 59	EASTERN CONSTELLATION	HADSON	F	12"	200	350	450
T 60	EASTERN CONSTELLATION	JAPAN	F	—	150	225	375
T 61	FARMAN TRIMOTOR	CK	W / U	10"	600	800	1200
T 62	F3H DEMON DOUGLAS	JAPAN	—	—	100	125	175
T 63	F3H DEMON MCDONNELL	JAPAN	F	—	75	100	125
T 64	F3F BIPLANE	CRAGSTAN	B / O	11½"	200	400	800
T 65	F3F BIPLANE	RICO	B / O	11½"	200	400	800
T 66	F9F GRUMMAN COUGAR	JAPAN	R / C	—	75	125	175
T 66A	F9F COUGAR	CRAGSTON	—	—	60	80	150
T 67	F9F-5 PANTHER	JAPAN	R / C	—	125	200	350
T 67A	F9F-5 PANTHER	JAPAN	B / O	—	150	225	400
T 68	F-14A TOMCAT	TN	B / O	12"	125	200	350
T 69	F-80 SINGLE PROP	BANDAI	F	4½"	50	75	125
T 70	F-84 AIRFORCE	LINEMAR	B / O	10"	100	150	200
T 71	F-86 USAF	JAPAN	F	—	75	125	195
T 72	F-86 USAF SABRE	JAPAN	F	—	75	125	195
T 73	F-90 LOCKHEED	BANDAI	F	4½"	15	30	55
T 74	F-90 (CELLULOID HEAD)	ASAHI	F	4½"	15	30	60
T 75	F-94 LOCKHEED STARFIRE	M	F	7"	25	50	90
T 76	FU-580	TT	F	7"	25	50	85
T 77	F-94C STARFIRE	Y	F	18"	150	300	475
T 78	F-94C STARFIRE	JAPAN	F	—	100	150	285
T 79	F-100 SUPER SABRE	JAPAN	B / O	—	125	225	350
T 80	F-100 C NAVY	ASAHI	—	—	100	150	225
T 81	F-100 SUPER SABRE	Y	—	—	75	125	200
T 82	F-100 SUPER SABRE	JAPAN	—	—	75	125	200
T 83	F-101 A VOODOO	S & E	F	—	150	300	450
T 84	F-102 USAF	HTS	F	11"	125	150	225
T 85	F-104 LOCKHEED	Y	F	16"	125	175	225
T 86	F-104 LOCKHEED	JAPAN	F	—	100	125	200
T 87	F-104 LOCKHEED FG 959	JAPAN	—	—	100	125	200
T 88	F-104 LOCKHEED 3581	KO	F	—	100	125	200
T 89	F-104 STARFIGHTER FG-956	Y	F	—	125	150	225
T 90	F-104 LOCKHEED FG-568	JAPAN	F	—	125	150	225

TYPE		MAN.	POWER	WINGSPAN	C6	C8	C10
T 91	FORD TRIMOTOR	TN	F	15″	100	150	300
T 92	FLYING TIGER DC 7	MARX	B / O	20″	175	300	400
T 93	FLYING BOAT NAVY AMPHIBIOUS	Y	CRANK	13″	600	900	1200
T 94	FIGHTER AIRPLANE	MARX	R / C	7″	25	50	85
T 95	F-COMETE FRENCH	FRANCE	W / U	12½″	150	225	350
T 96	FRENCH MONOPLANE	FRANCE	F	—	150	225	350
T 96A	FIAT CR-42 BIPLANE	INGAP	W / U	10″	800	1200	1800
T 97	GA-MTY	?	—	—		N P F	
T 98	GERMAN BIPLANE	TIPP	BATT/WU	20″	500	800	1600
T 99	GERMAN (SWASTIKA)	TIPP	BATT/WU	16″	900	1200	2000
T 100	HOKOKU SINGLE ENGINE	JAPAN	W / U	—	100	200	300
T 101	HK-555	W.GER	W / U	6″	20	40	90
T 102	HURRICANE A-25 BIPLANE	USAGIYA	F	—	50	90	150
T 103	HOSPITAL PLANE	TEKNO	P	14″	500	1000	1500
T 104	HEINZ 57 BURGER BLASTER (PROMO)	HEINZ	B / O	9½″		N P F	
T 105	JAPAN AIRLINES 747	JAPAN	—	—	100	200	300
T 106	JAPAN AIRLINES 727	JAPAN	—	—	100	200	300
T 107	JAPAN AIRLINES DC7	JAPAN	—	—	200	400	600
T 108	JAPAN AIRLINES DC7	JAPAN	—	—	200	400	600
T 109	JAPAN AIRLINES DC7	JAPAN	—	—	200	400	600
T 110	JAPAN AIRLINES CONCORDE	JAPAN	—	—	100	150	250
T 111	JENNY BIPLANE	HAJI	F	11½″	40	60	85
T 112	JENNY BIPLANE	S & E	F	14½″	90	135	195
T 113	JENNY BIPLANE	S & E	F	14½″	90	135	195
T 114	JENNY BIPLANE (RICKENBACKER)	JAPAN	F	14½″	120	200	275
T 115	JET COPTER	W.GER	F	8″	25	50	100
T 116	KAWANISHI K1-61 HEIN (TONY)	BANDAI	F	14″	100	200	400
T 117	KLM DC6	LINEMAR	F	—	150	275	450
T 118	KLM LOCKHEED CONSTELLATION	ARNOLD	F	—	300	450	785
T 119	LOCKHEED SIRIUS (LINDBERGH)	JAPAN	—	—	600	1200	1800
T 120	LOCKHEED USAF	JAPAN	F	8″	90	120	190
T 121	LOCKHEED CONSTRUCTION	ENG	—	22″	125	175	400
T 122	LIGHTED PISTON ACTION	G.W	B / O	15″	50	100	200
T 123	MARINE (F-106-?)	JAPAN	F	—	25	50	75
T 124	MATS USAF TRANSPORT	JAPAN	—	—	125	175	290
T 125	MARX MILITARY AEROPLANE	MARX	W / U	14″	80	120	250
T 126	MITSUBISHI ZERO (80s ISSUE)	JAPAN	F	15½″	75	100	150
T 127	MITSUBISHI ZERO	NOMURA	F	14″	150	275	400
T 128	MITSUBISHI ZERO	NOMURA	F	14″	150	275	400
T 129	MITSUBISHI ZERO	BANDAI	B / O	14″	150	300	450
T 130	MOUNT BLANC TRIMOTOR	FRANCE	W / U	21″	600	800	1200
T 131	NORTHWEST DC4	ASAHI	—	—	200	300	400
T 132	NORTHWEST DC-7C	Y	B / O	23½″	140	210	280
T 133	NP-001 JET FIGHTER	JAPAN	F	—	40	70	120
T 134	N-156 F NORTHROP	JAPAN	F	—	90	140	220
T 135	NORTHROP GAMA (PURE OIL) METALCRAFT	—	—	17″	400	800	1800
T 136	NAVY PROP	JAPAN	—	—	20	40	60
T 137	NAVY JET	Y	F	13″	90	120	200
T 138	PREWAR HI WING	JAPAN	W / U	—	500	1000	1500

TYPE		MAN.	POWER	WINGSPAN	C6	C8	C10
T 139	PREWAR HI WING	JAPAN	W / U	—	500	1000	1500
T 140	PAN AMERICAN	JAPAN	F	—	90	175	400
T 141	PAN AMERICAN CONSTELLATION	JAPAN	F	—	125	175	350
T 142	PAN AMERICAN DC-7C	Y	F	—	150	225	375
T 143	PAN AMERICAN DC-6	JAPAN	F	—	125	200	350
T 144	PAN AMERICAN 707	JAPAN	B / O	—	90	135	195
T 145	PAN AMERICAN DC-8	ATC	—	—	120	180	260
T 146	P-40 CURTISS WARHAWK	MARX	B / O	—	140	200	280
T 147	P-47 THUNDERBOLT	HTC	F	10 "	90	180	250
T 148	P-51 MUSTANG	HTC	F	10 "	100	210	375
T 149	RYANX2 SPIRIT OF ST LOUIS	LINEMAR	F	7 "	20	40	75
T 150	RYANX2 SPIRIT OF ST LOUIS	HTC	F	12 "	125	250	500
T 150A	RB-52 STATOFORTRESS	JAPAN	F	18 "	175	250	400
T 151	SPANISH TOP WING	RICO	W / U	7½ "	50	85	125
T 152	SPANISH TOP WING	PAYA	W / U	13¾ "	150	225	350
T 153	SPANISH WWII	PAYA	W / U	8¾ "	125	200	325
T 154	SPANISH TRIMOTOR	PAYA	W / U	9 "	150	250	450
T 155	SPANISH TRIMOTOR	PAYA	W / U	9 "	150	250	450
T 156	SPANISH 4 ENGINE # 158	RICO	W / U	13½ "	175	350	475
T 157	SPANISH 4 ENGINE # 158	RICO	W / U	13½ "	175	350	475
T 158	SPANISH LAR 2 ENGINE	RICO	W / U	13½ "	160	320	450
T 159	SPANISH FIGHTER # 160	RICO	W / U	7½ "	90	120	200
T 160	SPANISH SEAPLANE	RICO	W / U	13½ "	200	300	450
T 161	SABRE JET FIGHTER FW-100	TT	F	7 "	25	50	100
T 162	SEVEN SEAS DC-7C	DIAYA	F	10 "	75	125	225
T 163	SHOOTING FIGHTER "PHOENIX"	TN	B / O	9 "	30	60	125
T 164	SILVER MOON AMERICAN AIRLINES	BANDAI	F	10 "	100	175	250
T 165	SKYBIRD Mx2H "SPIRIT OF ST LOUIS"	BANDAI	F	9 "	75	125	175
T 166	SKY-GUARD	JAPAN	B / O	10 "	125	250	375
T 167	SKYCRUISER	MARX	F	14 "	30	60	125
T 168	SPITFIRE	HTC	F	10 "	80	150	225
T 169	STUKA JU 87	JEP	—	—	300	600	800
T 170	SUPER SONIC JET LINER	JAPAN	F	18 "	175	250	400
T 171	SUPER SONIC JETLINER	JAPAN	F	18 "	175	250	400
T 172	SV-3	MARX	F	6½ "	20	40	65
T 173	SWALLOW N-057	TM	R / C	9 "	60	110	225
T 174	TEMCO TT-1	JAPAN	F	—	150	225	300
T 175	TOKYO # 101 ROBIN	JAPAN	—	—		N P F	
T 176	TRAVEL AIR	BANDAI	F	9 "	75	120	190
T 176A	TWA TWIN ENGINE	JAPAN	W / U	6¾ "	95	150	225
T 177	TWIN TAIL SPARKLING JET	JAPAN	F	8 "	50	75	100
T 178	TWIN ENGINE	JAPAN	F	5 "	75	90	125
T 179	T-28 NORTHAMERICAN	BANDAI	B / O	9 "	100	250	375
T 180	UNITED MAINLINER	JAPAN	B / O	—	150	225	300
T 181	UN HOSPITAL PLANE	HTC	F	12 "	100	200	300
T 182	USAF PROP JET	JAPAN	F	—	90	120	175
T 183	USAF 4 ENGINE JET	JAPAN	F	—	120	175	225
T 184	USAF VERTICAL TAKE OFF	JAPAN	—	—	120	175	225
T 185	V-3 CH-548	HAJI	F	5½ "	20	40	65

TYPE		MAN.	POWER	WINGSPAN	C6	C8	C10
T 186	WWII FIGHTER	SPAIN	W / U	8½"	150	250	450
T 187	WWII FIGHTER	JAPAN	F	14½"	90	175	325
T 188	X-15 N.A.	S	F	10"	40	60	100
T 189	XF4D-1 DOUGLAS SKYRAY	JAPAN	F	—	40	60	80
T 190	X-36 USAF	JAPAN	F	—	60	80	100
T 191	XF-84H REPUBLIC	GW	B / O	15"	50	100	200
T 192	XF-160 MYSTERY ACTION	TN	B / O	11"	60	110	225

T 1

T 2

T 3

T 4-A

T 5

T 6

T 7

T 11 KULLIK COLLECTION

T 13

T12 KULLIK COLLECTION

T 15

T 14

T 19

T 20

T 21

T 22

T 23

T 24

T 25

T 26

T 27

T 28

T 29

T 30

T 31

104

T 32

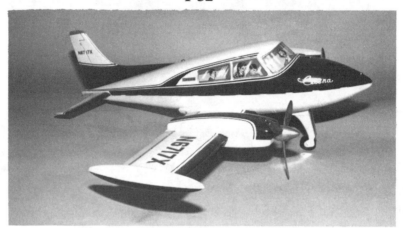

T 33

T 34

T 35

T 36   ABENSUR COLLECTION

CONDITION OF A TOY AND ITS RELATION TO PRICE
CONDITION CODE:

C6 - Good. Evident overall wear, well-played with, but acceptable to many collectors.

C8 - Very Good Minor wear overall, very clean.

C10 - Mint (like new).

Note: Mint in Box commands a higher price. Condition below C6 brings considerably lower prices.

T 37
ABENSUR COLLECTION

T 38

KULLIK COLLECTION

T 39

T 40   KULLIK COLLECTION

T 41

T 42

T 43

T 45

T 46

T 47

T 48

T-64, F3F Bi-plane.

T-40A, Cragstan Bi-plane 7F18.

(left) T-113, Jenny Bi-plane.

(right) T-112, Jenny Bi-plane.

T-96A, Fiat CR 42 Bi-plane.

(*left*) T-179, North American T-28.

(*right*) T-179, North American T-28.

T-150, Ryan X-2 Spirit of St. Louis.

T-168, Spitfire.

T-126, Mitsubishi Zero.

T-34A, Cessna HWN-70.

T-186, WWII Fighter.

T-187, WWII Navy Fighter.

T-148, P-51 Mustang.

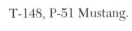

T-181, U.N. Hospital Plane.

T-99, German Army "Swastika."

T-57, Dehavilland Comet.

T-32, Cessna USAF 105.

T-147, P-47 Thunderbolt.

T-176A, TWA Twin Engine.

T-10, American Airlines
"Pamila."

T-103, Hospital Plane.

T-53, Douglas TriMotor.

T-121,
Lockheed Construction.

AM-1, Aero Mini A6M5 ZERO, Japanese Navy.

DK-85, Dinky HAWKER HURRICANE MK II C.

T-29, Bristol Bulldog.

DK-87, Dinky JUNKERS JU87B STUKA.

ED-10, Edison MACCHI CASTOLDI M.C. 72
low wing racer with floats.

T-56, Disney Comic Plane.

T-27, Bluebird Seaplane.

T-165, Skybird MX2H
Spirit of St. Louis.

T-35A, Cessna Twin Prop.

(left) TT-22, Tootsietoy
AERO-DAWN "UX-214".

(center) HU-10,
Hubley Lockheed-P-38
(2-piece casting).

(right) ER-1,
Erie NORTHROP GAMA
(2-piece casting).

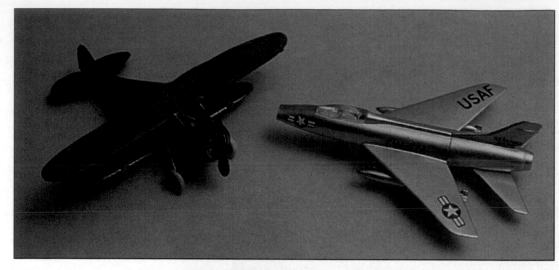

(left) TT-10, Tootsietoy WACO Bi-Plane "U.S. Navy".

(right) TK-11, Tekno SUPER SABRE F-100, "Danish/US Air Force".

(left) T-42, Tootsietoy SIKORSKY S:43, Coast Guard, 4 engine.

(right) TK-5, Tekno Twin Engine Hospital Plane (see Tinplate section for Tekno tin hospital plane).

(left) ER-3, Erie NORTHROP-DELTA (passenger).

(right) TT-19, Tootsietoy FORD TRIMOTOR.

(left) HU-5, Hubley U.S. ARMY low wing prop w/folding wheels.

(right) RN-1, Renwal TWA LOCKHEED CONSTELLA-TION.

T 49

T 51   KULLIK COLLECTION

T 52

T 53

T 54

T 55

T 56

T 57   **ABENSUR COLLECTION**

T 60

T 61

T 63

T 64

114

T 66-A

T 66

T 67

115

T 67-A

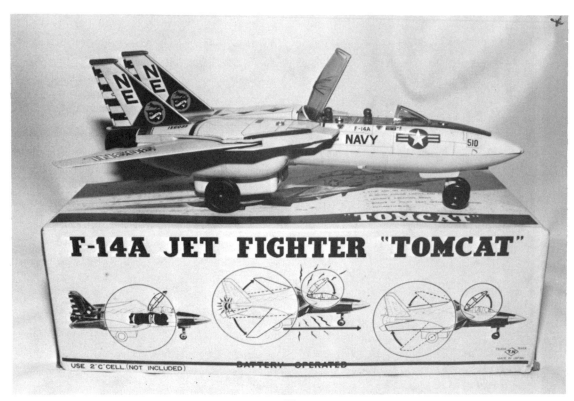

T 68

CONDITION OF A TOY AND ITS RELATION TO PRICE
CONDITION CODE:

C6 - Good. Evident overall wear, well-played with, but acceptable to many collectors.

C8 - Very Good Minor wear overall, very clean.

C10 - Mint (like new).

Note: Mint in Box commands a higher price. Condition below C6 brings considerably lower prices.

T 69

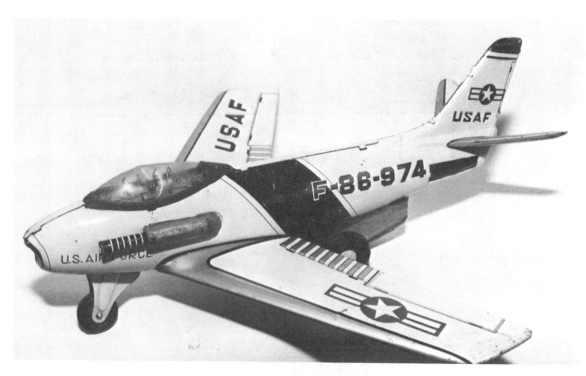

T 71

T 72

T 73
KULLIK COLLECTION

T 74
KULLIK COLLECTION

T 75

KULLIK COLLECTION

T 76

KULLIK COLLECTION

T 77

T 78

T 79

T 80

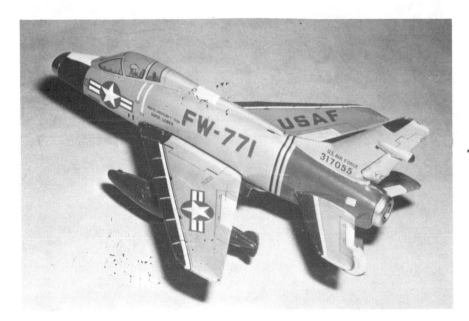

T 81

T 82

T 83

T 85

T 86

T 87

T 88

T 89

T 90

T 91

T 92

T 93

124

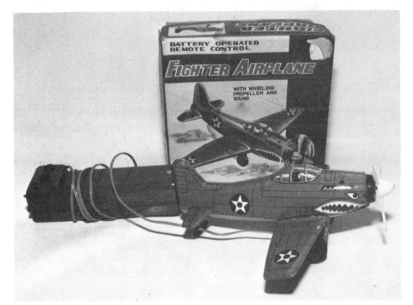

T 94   KULLIK COLLECTION

T 95   ABENSUR COLLECTION

T 96

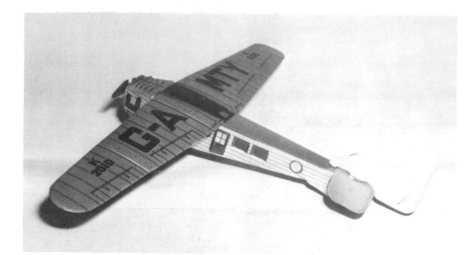

T 97

T 98

T 99

T 100

127

T 101   KULLIK COLLECTION

T 102

T 103

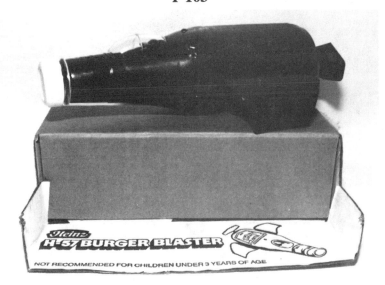

T 104   KULLIK COLLECTION

T 105

T 106

T 107

T 108

T 109

T 110

T 111

131

T 112

T 113

T 114

T 115
KULLIK COLLECTION

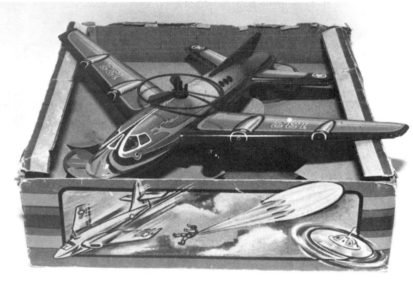

T 116

T 117

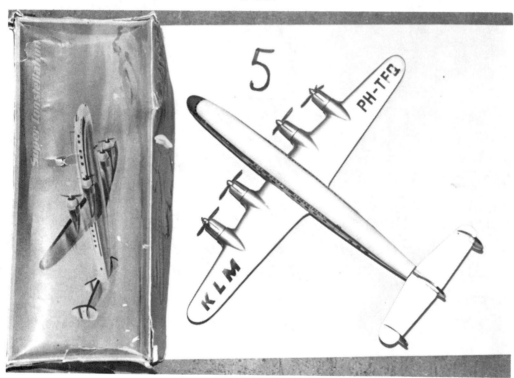

T 118

T 119

T 120

T 121

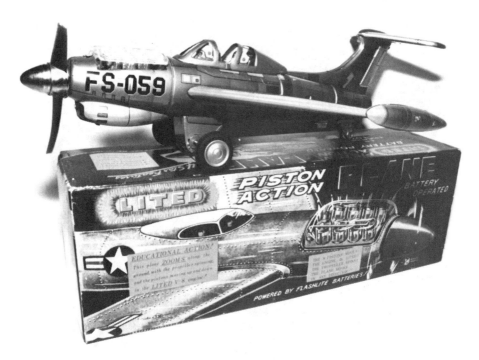

T 122

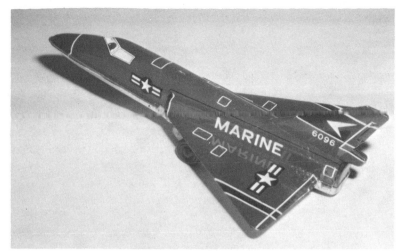

T 123

T 124

T 125   KULLIK COLLECTION

137

T 126

T 127

138

T 128

T 129

T 130   ABENSUR COLLECTION

T 131

T 132

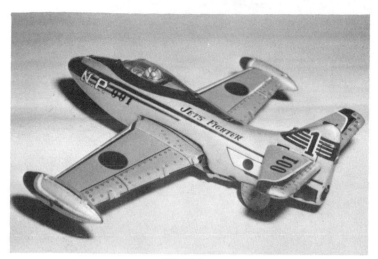

T 133

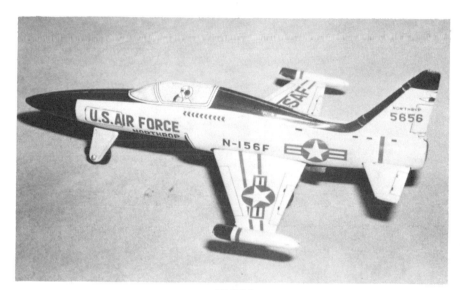

T 134

T 135

COLLECTION RICH SAVAGE

T 136

T 137

T 138

T 139

T 140

T 141

T 142

T 143

T 144

T 145

CONDITION OF A TOY AND ITS RELATION TO PRICE
CONDITION CODE:

C6 - Good. Evident overall wear, well-played with, but acceptable to many collectors.

C8 - Very Good Minor wear overall, very clean.

C10 - Mint (like new).

Note: Mint in Box commands a higher price. Condition below C6 brings considerably lower prices.

T 146 PHOTO COURTESY GERALD SHOOK

T 147

T 148

T 149   KULLIK COLLECTION

T 150

T 150-A

T 151
ABENSUR COLLECTION

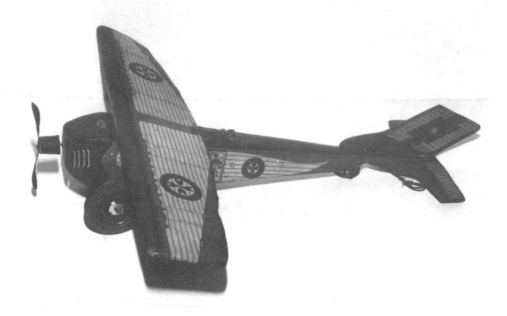

T 152   ABENSUR COLLECTION

T 153   ABENSUR COLLECTION

T 154   ABENSUR COLLECTION

T 155   ABENSUR COLLECTION

T 156
ABENSUR COLLECTION

T 157   ABENSUR COLLECTION

149

**T 158
ABENSUR COLLECTION**

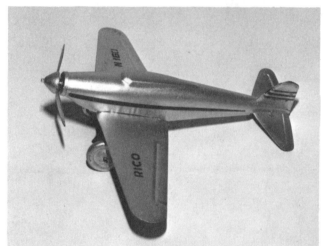

T 159   ABENSUR COLLECTION

**T 160·
ABENSUR COLLECTION**

T 161   KULLIK COLLECTION

T 162

CONDITION OF A TOY AND ITS RELATION TO PRICE
CONDITION CODE:

C6 - Good. Evident overall wear, well-played with, but acceptable to many collectors.

C8 - Very Good Minor wear overall, very clean.

C10 - Mint (like new).

Note: Mint in Box commands a higher price. Condition below C6 brings considerably lower prices.

T 163
KULLIK COLLECTION

T 164   ABENSUR COLLECTION

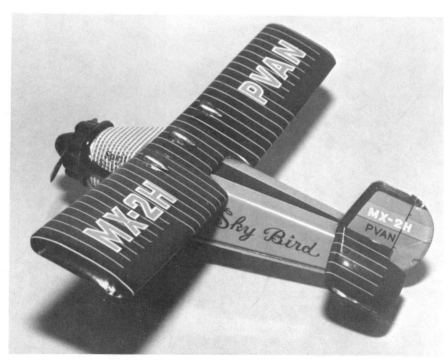

T 165

T 166

T 167   KULLIK COLLECTION

T 168

T 169

T 170

154

T 171

T 172
KULLIK COLLECTION

T 173
KULLIK COLLECTION

155

T 174

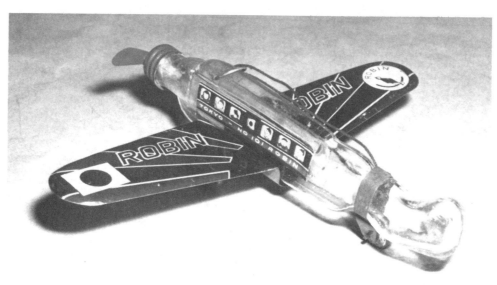

T 175

T 176

T 177   KULLIK COLLECTION

T 178

T 179

T 180

T 181

CONDITION OF A TOY AND ITS RELATION TO PRICE
CONDITION CODE:

C6 - Good. Evident overall wear, well-played with, but acceptable to many collectors.

C8 - Very Good Minor wear overall, very clean.

C10 - Mint (like new).

Note: Mint in Box commands a higher price. Condition below C6 brings considerably lower prices.

T 182

T 183

T 184

T 185 **KULLIK COLLECTION**

T 186

T 187

T 188   KULLIK COLLECTION

T 189

T 190

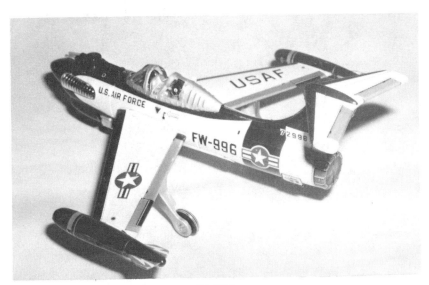

T 191

T 191

T 192   KULLIK COLLECTION

TIN HELICOPTERS

From The Bruce Kullik Collection

	TYPE	MAN.	POWER	WINGSPAN	C6	C8	C10
H 1	AIRFORCE RESCUE BATTALION	MARX	W / U	10½ "	65	85	125
H 2	ARMY H-8259	HAJI	R / C	12 "	25	45	65
H 2A	ARMY HELICOPTER	JAPAN	W / U	8	75	95	125
H 3	H-15	GAMA	F	5 "	20	35	50
H 4	HIGHWAY PATROL	JAPAN	F	8 "	20	35	50
H 5	H-2	TM	W / U	7 "	65	85	125
H 6	HELICOPTER	JAPAN	W / U	7½ "	100	150	200
H 7	HIGHWAY PATROL	K	F-	5 "	10	20	35
H 8	MERCURY 107 TWIN TURBINE	LINEMAR	F	9½ "	65	85	125
H 9	NEW YORK AIRWAYS	ALPS	D / O	13½ "	125	175	225
H 10	PIASECKI YH-16 HELICOPTER	Y	R / C	9 "	40	60	75
H 11	POLICE PATROL 107	JAPAN	F	12 "	40	60	75
H 12	PATROL HELICOPTER	TN	F	11 "	45	65	80
H 13	POLICE PATROL	SH	F	10½ "	30	50	70
H 14	PIASECKI ARMY MULE	RF	W / U	12 "	60	115	150
H 15	POLICE TRAFFIC CONTROL	MARUSAN	W / U	10½ "	65	85	125
H 16	PIASECKI HUP-2	TN	F	10½ "	50	75	100
H 17	PAN AM (PLASTIC) W.GER.	BEDICO	B / O	12 "		N P F	
H 18	RESCUE N7408	N	B / O	8½ "	50	75	100
H 19	RESCUE HELICOPTER 8556	KK	W / U	6 "	65	85	125
H 20	REMOTE CONTROL HELICOPTER	W.GER	W / U	8½ "	65	85	125
H 21	SIKORSKY 702	JAPAN	B / O	10 "	65	85	125
H 22	SORING COPTER	USA	PULL	10½ "	65	85	125
H 23	SABENA HELICOPTER S-58	CRAGSTON	B / O	12 "	100	150	200
H 24	SABENA NAVY	W.GER	R / W / U	9 "	90	125	175
H 25	TOY TOWN AIRWAYS	CHEIN	W / U	13 "	50	75	100
H 26	TRANSPORT HELICOPTER	DAIYA	F	9 "	25	40	65
H 27	US AIRFORCE WITH PISTON ACTION	TN	F	11 "	60	90	120
H 28	US ARMY	MARUSAN	W / U	10 "	30	50	75
H 29	WESTLAND N-57	ALPS	R / C	14 "	100	160	225
H 30	#68 (RED CROSS)	JAPAN	F	7 "	25	40	50

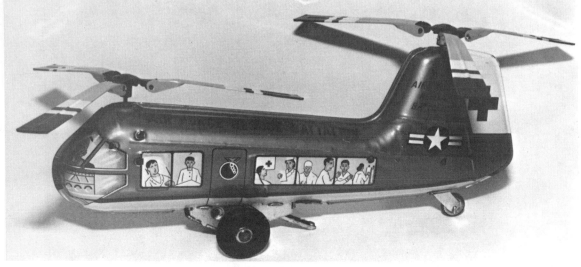

H 1

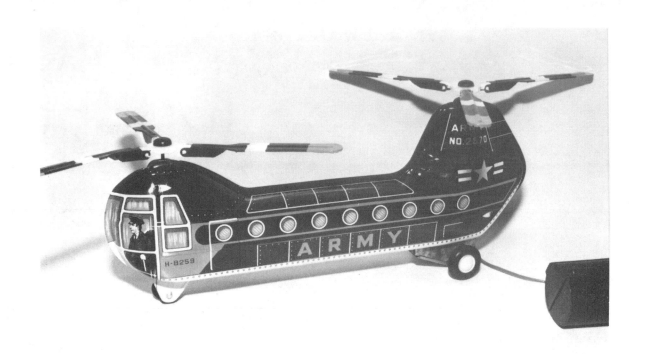

H 2

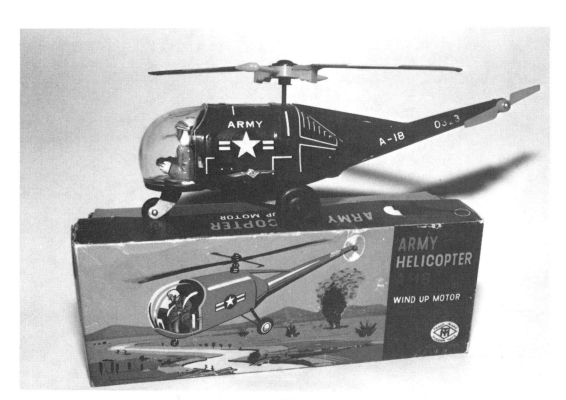

H 2-A

H 3

H 4

H 5

H 6

H 7

H 8

H 9

H 10

CONDITION OF A TOY AND ITS RELATION TO PRICE
CONDITION CODE:

C6 - Good. Evident overall wear, well-played with, but acceptable to many collectors.

C8 - Very Good Minor wear overall, very clean.

C10 - Mint (like new).

Note: Mint in Box commands a higher price. Condition below C6 brings considerably lower prices.

H 11

H 12

H 13

H 14

H 15

H 16

H 17

H 18

H 19

H 20

H 21

H 22

H 23

H 24

H 25

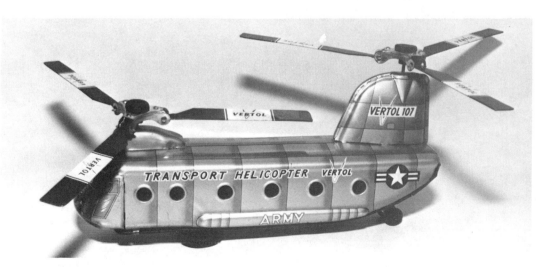

H 26

H 27

H 28

H 29

H 30

COX THIMBLE DROME AIRPLANES

List compiled by Danny Bynum

LM COX is the world's largest manufacturer of gas powered toys and small model engines. It all started in 1946 with the manufacture of wooden pop guns. The first metal toy produced was a 9½ " long racing car that small youngsters could roll on the floor or sidewalk. Soon thereafter, in 1947, COX introduced his first gas engine powered model race car that retailed for $19.95.

Model airplane production began in 1953 with the TD-1 and continues today with a wide variety of powered models. COX's trademark, "Thimble Drome," comes from the European name of an airport (air drome) and the diminutive size of the model powerplant, similar to a "thimble."

Because of the nature of the fuel used to power these models, condition of the plastic has to be considered. If the fuel and any fuel residue has been on the plastic for a period of time, staining will result. This staining is permanent and reduces the value of the model, thus the premium for new and unused examples, (C10).

Original boxes and packaging will add 20% to 30% to the C10 value depending on the condition of the box.

	MODEL	DESCRIPTION	YEARS	C6	C8	C10
CTD 1	TD-1	Red, yellow, blue, white (Skymaster), or a combination of each color w/aluminum wing. Has die cast TD engine w/plastic tank.	1953-1959	45	85	165
CTD 2	TD-3	White, yellow w/Thimble Drome engine w/plastic tank.	1954-1958	35	55	115
CTD 3	TD-3 "Flying Circus"	White w/Red Checkerboard Wing. Engine w/Metal tank.	1958-1961	35	45	95
CTD 4	TD-4 "Flight Trainer"	Red/Blue, Blue/Yellow	1956-1959	35	45	75
CTD 5	SUPER CUB 105 (TD)	Yellow (w/Inverted Engine)	1957-1960	25	55	75
		"Civil Air Patrol" Version (Yellow & Blue)	1959-1961	30	55	90
CTD 6	LIL STINKER (TD)	Red/White Bi-Plane w/.020 Engine	1958-1964	25	45	70
CTD 7	SUPER SABRE F-100 (TD)	White or Grey w/.020 Engine	1958-1963	35	55	95
CTD 8	P-40 FLYING TIGER (TD)	Tan & Marked "Flying Tiger" on Fuselage (w/Inverted Engine)	1959-1960	35	55	95
CTD 9	COMANCHE	Tan/Cream, Maroon/Chrome with .15 Engine	1960-1964	45	75	125
CTD 10	CURTISS PUSHER	Black & Orange Wright Brothers Bi-Plane	1960-1962	35	70	95
CTD 11	PT-19	Blue/Yellow (There are many different versions of the PT-19. The first one is with an open front nose allowing the engine to slide through the front.	1960-1965	20	35	55
		The 2nd version has a bar across the nose.	1966-1976	15	25	40
		The 3rd version has a non-integral tank located in the fuselage. The last versions are models with pilot, windscreen variations and plastic gas tank.	1977-1994	15	20	30
CTD 12	P-40 WARHAWK	Tan w/inverted engine and painted pilot.	1961-1968	25	45	75
		Tan w/upright engine and painted pilot.	1968-1971	20	35	65
		Tan w/green or black camoflage.	1969-1970	30	40	60
		Green w/camoflage and metal tank engine until 1978	1971-1978	20	30	55
		Green w/camoflage with a plastic tank in fuselage	1978-1991	20	30	45
CTD 13	SUPER CUB 150	Red and Cream (Upright engine has metal tank)	1961-1962	25	45	75

MODEL		DESCRIPTION	YEARS	C6	C8	C10
		Red and Cream (w/plastic tank in fuselage)	1963-1965	20	35	60
		Red and Cream (w/plastic wheel pants)	1963-1965	25	30	55
CTD 14	AVION SHINN	Yellow	1962	35	65	110
CTD 15	STUKA	Green (w/molded landing gear)	1962-1965	30	50	95
CTD 16	P-51 BENDIX RACER	Red, Yellow (w/molded landing gear)	1963-1964	35	65	115
CTD 17	ARMY P-51B MUSTANG	Olive Drab (w/molded landing gear and razorback fuse)	1963-1970	25	35	65
CTD 18	NAVY HELLDRIVER	Light Blue, Dark Blue	1963-1966	35	55	95
CTD 19	L-4 GRASSHOPPER	Olive drab Army Piper Cub	1963-1970	25	45	75
CTD 20	RAF SPITFIRE	Light green w/camoflage	1964-1965	35	55	95
		Dark green w/camoflage	1966-1969	25	40	75
CTD 21	KITTY HAWK SPITFIRE	Green w/yellow tail and lettering	1964-1965	35	60	100
CTD 22	SPOOK	White flying wing kit w/engine	1964	25	55	85
CTD 23	A-25 DIVE BOMBER	Olive drab	1965-1967	35	65	120
CTD 24	STUKA	Black with landing gear molded into wing	1965-1981	30	45	85
		Black with landing gear bolted onto wing	1981-1987	25	40	70
		Black w/bolt on gear and upright engine.	1987-1989	25	35	60
CTD 25	T-28 TRAINER	Yellow	1966-1967	25	45	85
CTD 26	QZ PT-19	Red/white (Quite Zone)	1966-1969	25	45	60
CTD 27	AD-6 SKYRAIDER	Tan, White, Blue	1967-1969	25	45	75
CTD 28	NAVY CORSAIR	Blue	1968-1972	25	45	60
CTD 29	PITTS SPECIAL	White .020 powered bi-plane	1968 only	25	45	85
CTD 30	CORSAIR	THOMPSON TROPHY RACER-Red	1969-1970	30	45	75
CTD 31	MINI STUNT	Lime green Bi-Plane w/.020 engine 1969	1969-1970	25	45	75
CTD 32	RYAN PT-20	Army olive drab/yellow (.020 engine)	1969-1970	35	45	65
CTD 33	RYAN ST-3	White/blue w/.020 engine & 2 pilots	1969-1970	35	45	65
CTD 34	CORSAIR II	Chrome w/red & white checkerboard on wing	1970-1972	30	45	65
CTD 35	RED KNIGHT	Dark red Bi-plane w/.020 engine	1970-1972	25	45	60
CTD 36	P-51D MUSTANG	Olive drab (w/bubble canopy and bolt on landing gear	1971-1978	25	35	50
CTD 37	MISS AMERICA P-51	Red/White/Blue-1st version w/molded gear	1971-1972	30	45	50
		Red/White/Blue-2nd version w/bolt on landing gear	1972-1975	25	35	45
CTD 38	RIVETS RACER	Red/yellow with Pilot Figure	1971-1973	30	40	60
CTD 39	ACRO PIPER CUB	Orange/White	1971-1972	25	35	50
CTD 40	SOPWITH CAMEL	Yellow/Blue	1972-1974	20	30	50
CTD 41	FOKKER D-7	Red/Blue	1972-1974	20	30	50
CTD 42	FOKKER TRIPLANE	Red	1973-1974	25	35	55
CTD 43	BUSHMASTER	Red/White (w/pontoons and skis)	1973-1974	25	40	60
CTD 44	FI-SPORT TRAINER	Pink w/Blue Canopy	1973-1981	20	30	45
CTD 45	SUPER STUNTER	Black/Blue	1974-1979	20	30	40
CTD 46	SKY-COPTER	Yellow/Orange w/metal tanked engine	1975-1976	20	35	45
		Yellow/Orange w/plastic gas tank	1976-1979	15	30	40
CTD 47	SUPER CHIPMUNK	Red/White/Blue	1975-1982	20	30	40
CTD 48	P-51 MUSTANG	Grey w/WWII Invasion Stripes & side mounted engine	1975-1977	15	25	40
CTD 49	CRUSADER	White/Blue	1976-1979	15	25	40

MODEL		DESCRIPTION	YEARS	C6	C8	C10
SURE FLYER SERIES						
CTD 50	P-39 AIRCOBRA	Blue	1976-1979	10	20	35
CTD 51	SKYMASTER	Orange	1976-1979	10	20	35
CTD 52	CESSNA 150	White	1976-1978	10	20	35
CTD 53	PIPER COMANCHE	White	1976-1977	10	20	35
E-Z FLYER SERIES						
CTD 54	AEROBAT 150	White (1988-1993) Yellow w/muffler (1993-1995)	1988-1995	10	15	25
CTD 55	FIREBIRD	Red w/muffler	1993-1995	10	15	25
CTD 56	THUNDERBOLT	Black w/muffler	1993-1995	10	15	25
WINGS SERIES						
CTD 57	FALCON	White	1977-1979	10	15	25
CTD 58	HUSTLER	Red	1977-1977	10	15	25
CTD 59	MANTIS	Yellow	1977-1979	10	15	25
CTD 60	F-15 EAGLE	White	1977-1979	10	15	25
CTD 61	BLACK MANTIS	Black	1979	10	15	25
CTD 62	EAGLE	White	1980-1981	10	15	25
CTD 63	RED DEVIL	Red	1980	10	15	25
CTD 64	NIGHT WING	Black	1980-1981	10	15	25
CTD 65	BARON	Black	1980-1981	10	15	25
CTD 66	RED WING RACER	Red	1981 only	15	20	30
CTD 67	DELTA F-15	Grey	1981-1986	10	15	25
CTD 68	BLUE ANGEL	Blue	1982-1986	10	15	25
CTD 69	PHANTOM 5	Green	1982-1986	10	15	25
CTD 70	STAR CRUISER	White (Flying saucer)	1978-1979	20	25	35
CTD 71	SPITFIRE	Light blue (Reissue)	1979-1980	20	30	40
CTD 72	P-51 MUSTANG	Olive drab (w/side mount engine)	1979-1980	20	30	35
CTD 73	STARFIGHTER	White (Buck Rogers series)	1980 only	20	35	50
CTD 74	INVADER	Black (Buck Rogers series flying saucer)	1980 only	20	35	45
CTD 75	SKY-RANGER	White (Helicopter)	1980-1989	15	25	35
CTD 76	SOPWITH CAMEL	Tan/Blue	1981 only	15	25	45
CTD 77	P-51 MUSTANG	Grey (w/upright engine)	1981-1990	15	20	25
CTD 78	PT-19	Red/white	1981-1984	15	25	40
CTD 79	P-51 MUSTANG	Red Baron	1981 only	20	35	55
CTD 80	SUPER SPORT II	Yellow	1982-1990	10	20	30
CTD 81	SKY COMMANDO	Green man w/red rotors	1983 only	15	25	50
CTD 82	P-39 AIRCOBRA	Tan (reissue)	1986-1994	15	20	30
CTD 83	CESSNA 150	White (reissue)	1986-1995	15	20	30
CTD 84	COSMIC WIND	Red	1986-1989	15	20	35
CTD 85	AIRWOLF	Black Helicopter	1987-1989	15	25	40
CTD 86	STEALTH BOMBER	Black	1987-1989	15	25	35
CTD 87	COMANCHE	White (reissue)	1987-1992	15	20	30
CTD 88	TOP GUN	Grey	1988-1990	15	20	30
CTD 89	SUPER CHIPMUNK	White/red (reissue)	1988-1993	15	20	30
CTD 90	SKY-JUMPER	Olive drab Helicopter	1989-1995	15	20	35
CTD 91	UFO FLYING SAUCER	White	1990-1991	10	15	25
CTD 92	MISS AMERICA P-51	Red/White/Blue (reissue) w/wire landing gear	1990-1991	15	20	35

MODEL		DESCRIPTION	YEARS	C6	C8	C10
CTD 93	SOPWITH CAMEL	Olive green/cream (reissue)	1990-1991	15	20	30
CTD 94	FOKKER DVII	Blue grey/light grey (reissue)	1990-1991	15	20	30
CTD 95	FOKKER TRIPLANE	Red (reissue)	1990-1991	15	25	35
CTD 96	DESERT DEFENDER	Tan	1991-1993	15	20	25
CTD 97	FA-18 HORNET	Light grey	1991-1995	10	20	30
CTD 98	BLUE ANGEL	Blue	1990-1995	10	20	30
CTD 99	ATTACK COBRA	Black Helicopter	1993-1995	10	15	25
CTD 100	MARINE CORSAIR	Blue	1994-1995	10	15	25
CTD 101	ME-109 STUNT FLYER	White & Black w/Styrofoam Wing	1994-1995	10	15	25

CTD 8

CONDITION OF A TOY AND ITS RELATION TO PRICE
CONDITION CODE:

C6 - Good. Evident overall wear, well-played with, but acceptable to many collectors.

C8 - Very Good Minor wear overall, very clean.

C10 - Mint (like new).

Note: Mint in Box commands a higher price. Condition below C6 brings considerably lower prices.

CTD 11

CTD 12

CTD 12

CTD 18

CTD 20

CTD 23

CTD 24

CTD 25

183

CTD 28

CTD 40

CTD 41

CTD 53

CTD 54

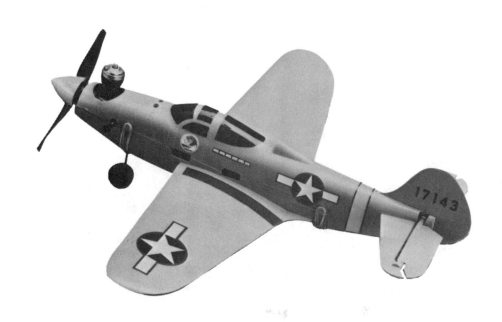

CTD 55

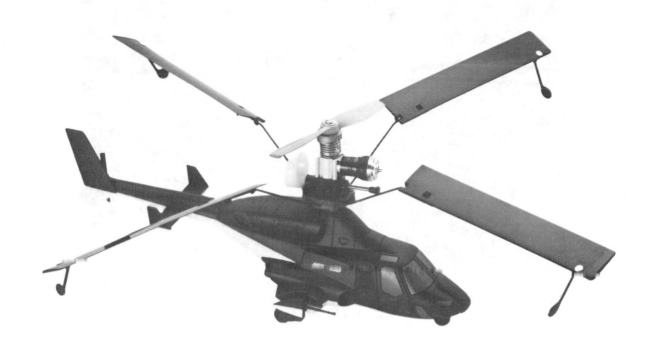

CTD 85

CTD 86

CTD 96

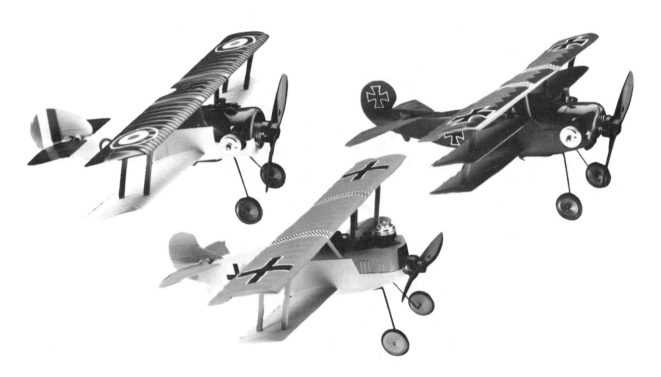

CTD 93 **CTD 94** **CTD 95**

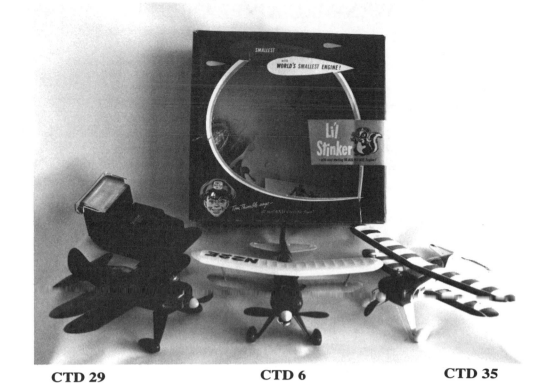

CTD 29   **CTD 6**   **CTD 35**

CONDITION OF A TOY AND ITS RELATION TO PRICE
CONDITION CODE:

C6 - Good. Evident overall wear, well-played with, but acceptable to many collectors.

C8 - Very Good Minor wear overall, very clean.

C10 - Mint (like new).

Note: Mint in Box commands a higher price. Condition below C6 brings considerably lower prices.

WEN-MAC AIRPLANES

WenMac is credited with being the first US company to produce and sell a complete plastic "Ready-To-Fly" model airplane complete with engine. There is some disagreement as to which model was issued first, the Aeromite with the Anderson "Baby Spitfire" engine, or the "Night Fighter" with a WenMac produced engine. Early advertising indicates that the Night Fighter was available first.

In later years WenMac was acquired by the AMF (American Machine & Foundry) Corporation. The airplanes produced under AMF are marked with both WenMac and AMF. Eventually, AMF ended production of the popular line of model airplanes and WenMac ceased to exist.

	MODEL # & NAME	COLORS	YEARS	C6	C8	C10
WM 1	AEROMITE	Black w/"Baby Spitfire" Engine	1950-1953	35	55	95
WM 2	NIGHT FIGHTER	Blue w/WenMac Engine	1952-1955	35	50	85
WM 3	100-AEROMITE	Red, Blue, Yellow, Black, Chrome	1956-1964	25	40	75
WM 4	103-BASIC TRAINER	Red, Blue, Yellow, Black, Chrome	1962-1964	35	45	85
WM 5	105-TURBOJET	Red & Cream, Red & Chrome	1958-1964	25	40	75
WM 6	110-BEECHCRAFT M-35	Blue, Green, Yellow, White	1958-1964	25	40	75
WM 7	115-FLYING PLATFORM	Olive Drab W/USN Emblems	1956-1958	35	65	95
WM 8	120-CUTLASS-NAVY	Blue, Black, Yellow-Rear Engine	1958-1960	35	45	75
WM 9	121-FAN/JET XL600	Red Delta Wing W/Rear Engine	1958-1960	35	45	75
WM 10	122-P-26 PURSUIT	Blue/Yellow	1958-1962	35	65	135
WM 11	130-EARTH SATELLITE	Red Flying Saucer	1960-1964	25	45	65
WM 12	145-P-38 Lightning	Red, Grey, Tan, Chrome W 2 Engines	1959-1964	35	65	125
WM 13	US ARMY HOVERCRAFT	Olive Drab	1960-1964	25	40	65
WM 14	180-B-33 DEBONAIR	Green, Yellow, Chrome	1962-1964	30	45	70
WM 15	170-SBD-5 NAVY DIVE BOMBER	Dark Blue	1962-1964	25	45	85
WM 16	155-A-24 ARMY ATTACK BOMBER	Olive Drab	1962-1964	25	45	85
WM 17	175-MARINE SCOUT BOMBER	Yellow & Orange	1962-1964	25	45	85
WM 18	108-RCAF BANSHEE RAIDER	Black	1963-1964	30	45	90

VACUM FORMED:

WM 19	160-GIANT P-51 MUSTANG	White	1959-1960	25	40	65
WM 20	165-GIANT P-40 FLYING TIGER	White	1959-1960	25	40	65
WM 21	142-CESSNA 175 TRAINER	Red/White	1962-1964	25	40	60

CORSAIR:

WM 22	115-MARINE CORSAIR	Red	1958-1964	25	40	65
WM 23	125-NAVY CORSAIR	Blue	1958-1964	25	40	65
WM 24	135-YELLOW JACKET CORSAIR	Yellow	1959-1964	25	40	65
	F4U MARINE FIGHTER CORSAIR	Chrome	1959-1962	25	40	75

P-39 & P-63:

WM 25	150-P-39 AIR COBRA	Olive Drab	1962-1964	25	45	70
WM 26	185-P-63 KING COBRA	Chrome	1962-1964	25	45	75
WM 27	153-RAF DAY FIGHTER	White	1963-1964	25	45	70

MODEL # & NAME	COLORS	YEARS	C6	C8	C10
FLYING WINGS:					
WM 28 THUNDERBIRD	Light Blue/White	1963-1964	20	40	65
WM 29 HAWK	Yellow/White	1963-1964	20	40	65
WM 30 ALBATROSS	Red/White/Blue	1963-1964	20	40	65
WM 31 EAGLE	Red/White/Blue	1963-1964	20	40	65
WM 32 FALCON	Red/White/Blue	1963-1964	20	40	65
WM 33 BAT	Red/White/Blue	1963-1964	20	40	65
WM 34 STUNT TRAINER	Red/Yellow	1963-1964	20	40	65
WM 35 118-MARINE CORPS TRAINER	Yellow	1963-1964	25	45	75
WM 36 117-NAVY SNJ-3	Light Blue	1963-1964	25	45	75
WM 37 115-AT-6	Olive Drab	1963-1964	25	45	75
WM 38 116-NAVY SNJ-3	Chrome	1963-1964	25	45	75

WM 14

WM 25

WM 26

WM 38

TOY AIRPLANE COLLECTORS

NAME	SPECIALTY
Ron Smith 33005 Arlesford Solon, Ohio 44139 216-248-7066	Tin Biplanes Tin WWII Fighter Planes Japanese Tin Cars
Martin Braunlich 428 E 328th Street Willowick, Ohio 44095 216-943-0712	Dinky and Mercury Airplanes ID. Models
Bruce Kullik 13125 Forest Road Burton, Ohio 44021 216-635-0371	All Japanese Tin Aircraft Plus Helicopters
Danny Bynum 12311 Wedgehill Lane Houston, Texas 77077 713-531-5711	Gas Powered Aircraft and Cars
Rich Savage 9690 Brookstone Way Strongsville, Ohio 44136 216-238-7255	Tootsytoy Airplane or Auto Boxed Sets
Rodney Abensur 4 Chemin Des Chavannes 1247 Anieres, Geneva Switzerland	Japanese Tin Police, Fire and Taxies Tin Motorcycles

PUBLICATIONS

Plane News
P.O. Box 845
Greenwich, CT 06836
203-629-5270

Quarterly, Color
$35.00 Year Subscription
All Airplanes

Antique Toy World
P.O. Box 34509
Chicago, IL 60634
312-725-0633

Monthly, B/W and Color
$39.95 Year Subscription
Some Airplanes, Mostly
Antique Toys

Captain's Log
World Airline Historical Society
13739 Piscarsa Drive
Jacksonville, FL 32225
904-221-1446

Quarterly B/W
$20.00 Year Subscription
Airline and Airport
Histories, Memorabilia
Items

Gas Toy Collector
P.O. Box 440818
Houston, Texas 77244-0818
713-531-5711

Monthly, B/W
Subscription Rates
USA $15.00 Canda $17.00
Foreign $20.00 Per Year
Sample Issue $1.00

WANTED

Your cast iron or pressed steel airplane
for our second edition of
Collecting Toy Airplanes.
Send us a good 35mm print with
Manufacture, Aircraft Name, Size
and Approximate C-10 Value
include your name on the back
of the photo.
You will receive photo credit.
If you have a tin plate or diecast airplane
not pictured or listed, it will be
included in second edition.

Ron Smith
33005 Arlesford Drive
Solon, Ohio 44139

THE IDEAL PRODUCT FOR PLASTIC
and PAINTED METAL TOYS!

2 ounce kit (1&2) is only **$5.95** plus $1.75 shipping.
8 ounce kit (1&2) is only **$12.95** plus $3.00 shipping.

AVION HOBBY PRODUCTS
P.O. BOX 440818
HOUSTON, TX 77244-0818